Copyright © 2008 by Bramcost Publications
All rights reserved
Published in the United States of America

This Bramcost Publications edition is an unabridged republication of the rare original work first published in 1926.

www.BramcostPublications.com

ISBN 10: 1-934268-86-0
ISBN 13: 978-1-934268-86-5

Library of Congress Control Number: 2008938930

MILLINERY

BY

JANE LOEWEN

Formerly Millinery Instructor at the University
of Chicago ; Originator of Jane Hedden
Hat Patterns ; Author of Numerous
Works and Articles on Millinery and Designing

PREFACE

THERE has always been a feeling among women that millinery was something beyond their power of accomplishment, that the construction of hats required a great amount of creative ability and highly specialized training. This belief has been fostered by two factors: first, the pathetic creations that many women have perpetrated when trying to make their own hats; second, the professional milliner's attitude. The latter has always encouraged the idea that great talent and highly specialized training are necessary for the successful making of hats. This has been done for evident trade reasons.

Two things, creative talent and special training, are necessary for anyone to become a real designer of hats. But the nonprofessional or home woman need not be a designer. There are not fifty actual style originators in the United States and France together. Most milliners and trimmers are merely specialized adapters of ideas.

Any home girl or woman with average good taste and judgment can very quickly learn to copy or adapt the styles she sees in shop or style magazine to suit her own needs.

Knowledge of millinery principles and processes of construction she does need, as does any professional worker. This knowledge is not so deep and difficult of attainment but that any girl of average intelligence can master it.

For the student there are these things to remember: no true craftsman is ever satisfied with any work which falls short of perfection; there is no creative work, whether it be music, painting, cooking, or sewing, in which one attains perfection without practice; one learns more from applying principles than from mere perusal of them. Many times instructions which seem difficult at first reading are very simple when followed step by step.

The object of this book is to so classify and set forth the practical and technical principles of millinery that a working knowledge of it will be easily within the grasp of the student.

JANE LOEWEN

CONTENTS

CHAPTER		PAGE
I.	WIRE FRAMES	1

Uses of wire frames — Mathematical side of frame making — Process of constructing a wire frame for a hat — Dimensions for standard hats — Questions

| II. | MOLDED FRAMES | 17 |

Molded or pressed frames — Hand-molded frames — Bias dry-molded frames — Questions

| III. | PATTERN FRAMES | 29 |

Classification of frames made from patterns — Comparison of processes in making unrolled and rolled brims — Cutting the frame — Wiring frame — Binding a frame — Covering frame with interlining — Questions

| IV. | CROWNS | 40 |

Frame foundations used for crowns — Kinds of crowns — Outline of kinds of crowns and their appropriate brims — How to determine kinds of crowns suitable to individual types of faces — Questions

| V. | STAPLE MILLINERY MATERIALS | 52 |

Materials used — Questions

| VI. | CUTTING MATERIALS | 64 |

Cutting a true bias — Cutting a long bias — Table of bias measures — Rules for measuring material for a bias that is to be stretched — Correct shading for velvet and soleil — Measuring a frame for the correct amount of material — Accuracy in cutting, a large factor in cost saving — Methods used for cutting maline — Cutting bias binding from frame and crown edges — Questions

| VII. | THE FABRIC HAT | 71 |

Fall materials and fabrics — Classified construction of fabric hats for fall and winter — Questions

CONTENTS

VIII.	BRAID HATS	91
	Kinds — Manner of sewing — Questions	
IX.	TRANSPARENT HATS	101
	Kinds — Preparing the frame — Edge finishes — Appropriate trimmings — Questions	
X.	DRAPED HATS	123
	Matrons' turbans — Harem turbans — Draped tams — Section hats — Questions	
XI.	TAILORED TRIMMINGS	136
	Severe, factory-tailored hats — Semitailored hats — Kinds of tailored trimmings — Questions	
XII.	DRESS-HAT TRIMMINGS	154
	Trimmings for which the hat is a background — Trimming which is part of the design — Questions	
XIII.	CLEANING AND REMODELING	168
	Cleaning — Remodeling — Questions	
XIV.	COLOR HARMONY AS APPLIED TO THE INDIVIDUAL .	177
	Purpose of color in adorning the person — Color *versus* temperament — Chart of color combinations suitable to various types — Questions	
XV.	LINE HARMONY	184
	Fundamental principles of line — Principles of line as applied to the individual — Questions	

MILLINERY

MILLINERY

CHAPTER I

WIRE FRAMES

INTRODUCTION
I. USES OF WIRE FRAMES
   Wire frames for molding
   1. Elastic molded over a wire frame
   2. Buckram molded over a wire frame
   3. Willow molded over a wire frame
   Wire frames for transparent hats
   1. Frames for transparent lace hats
   2. Frames for transparent maline hats
   3. Frames for hair-braid hats
   Wire-frame uses to be avoided

II. MATHEMATICAL SIDE OF FRAME MAKING
   Mathematical principles involved
   Mathematical accuracy
   Enlarging or reducing dimensions
   1. A larger edge wire
   2. A smaller edge wire
   3. Larger headsize
   4. Smaller headsize

III. PROCESS OF CONSTRUCTING A WIRE FRAME FOR A HAT
   Correct order of recording measurements
   Getting correct headsize
   Geometrical precision required
   1. Marking the headsize for brace position
   2. Mounting the brace wire
   3. Marking the brace wire for correct measurements

IV. DIMENSIONS FOR STANDARD HATS
    Medium rolled brim
    Medium small poke
    Child's poke
QUESTIONS

INTRODUCTION

The making of wire frames comes first in the many steps involved in hat construction because the original mold for any hat or hat frame is made of wire. Therefore, wire frames are made the subject of our first chapter.

For practical beginner's work, however, a wire frame is a very poor first lesson, as they are difficult to make until the student has learned to manipulate millinery materials. The wise plan is to have the students familiarize themselves with Chapters I and II by reading only and to begin actual hat construction with pattern frames, Chapter III.

Students who have only a brief millinery course and short class periods for a few semesters should not attempt wire frames. They are, however, very necessary for anyone who means to make much of millinery or to train for professional work.

I. USES OF WIRE FRAMES

WIRE FRAMES FOR MOLDING

Wire frames always suggest transparent hats, but to the milliner their greatest importance is for workroom use as molds over which to stretch handmade frames (see Chapter II).

The designer of original models shapes the wire frame. A maker usually prepares the frame ready for the shaping and edge wire and braces it with brace wires tied at very close intervals.

After the designer gives the outline and the maker ties in the brace wires, it is ready for the frame material to be stretched over it or to use as a model for braid sewing.

If a French hat or any model hat of rolled or irregular brim is to be copied, a wire frame is made first. A wire headsize is made with long brace wires (see section III of this chapter). This wire headsize is slipped inside the hat headsize and the wires bent back over the hat and shaped exactly like it. The edge wire may be tied on to the cross braces and enough round brace wires tied on (but not cut) to give the exact shape of the hat.

Care must be exercised not to get the wire frame larger than the hat because the willow or elastic stretched over it is naturally a little larger than the wire frame when finished.

A willow or elastic net frame stretched over a wire frame made in this way will give more exact duplication of a shape than any other frame can.

1. Elastic molded over a wire frame. Elastic net makes a soft frame with a good deal of body to it and is desirable for stretching turbans, small frames, and medium brims. There is no other frame material which is so soft and yet holds its shape so well.

2. Buckram molded over a wire frame. Buckram makes a much stiffer frame, one which will stand a great deal of handling in the making. While it is easier for the amateur milliner to handle, it will break more easily when worn than will an elastic net frame, and is never so comfortable as a softer frame.

There are two grades of buckram, one rather heavy grade which is commonly sold when one merely asks for buckram, and a much lighter grade called jockey buckram. Jockey makes a good frame on which to sew straw braid. It makes a good foundation for velvet and any material with a nap. If crêpe, taffeta, or satin is used on a stretched buckram frame, an interlining must always be used or the hat is hard-looking.

3. Willow molded over a wire frame. Willow, when a good quality can be obtained, is the most satisfactory material for stretching large and irregular brims. It really is a two-ply or double-frame material. One ply of it is a fine, lightweight crinoline. The other is a pliable weave of willow fiber. The two materials are sized (or starched) and dried together. The willow gives stiffness, the crinoline gives it body.

The better grades of willow are made in Switzerland and France. During the war none was imported to America. The only thing obtainable was a much inferior quality which came from Japan.

It is still almost impossible to get the better grade of willow. In many workrooms milliners have given up trying to use the Japanese quality, and elastic net or one thickness of elastic net and one of cape net are used instead. The Japanese use a quality of fiber which is either so brittle that it breaks under the most careful handling or so soft that the frame will not hold its shape.

Wire Frames for Transparent Hats

The fewer round braces that can be used for a transparent hat the softer and more attractive looking it will be. A sprung-steel edge wire makes a truer outline and eliminates the need of round brace wires (see Figure 3).

1. Frames for transparent lace hats. Transparent lace hats are divided into two classes according to the edge finishes used.

Soft extended lace edges. The finished edge of the lace from which the hat is made is extended beyond the edge wire, giving an irregular and draped effect. For this type of hat the edge wire must be wrapped (or wound) with maline as a finish and as something to sew to. The brace wires are also wrapped unless a maline underfacing is used (see Chapter IX, section II).

Fold edges of fabric. A bias fold of velvet, soleil, silk, or maline is sewn to the frame edge. This may be extended beyond the edge wire, giving a soft edge, or it may be turned back over the top of the hat in a more tailored fashion.

In either case an underfacing is used and the wires need not be wrapped.

2. Frames for transparent maline hats. The wire frame for a soft or shirred maline hat is made in the same way as one for a soft lace hat (see Chapter IX, section II).

The wire frame for a fitted maline hat (see Chapter IX, page 110) must have more braces than one for a soft hat.

When maline is fitted on a wire frame, more braces are necessary to keep the maline from falling out of shape between the wires.

If a fitted-fabric edge flange is used, frame net or crinoline must first be fitted in place (see Figure 48, Chapter IX).

3. Frames for hair-braid hats. Wire frames for transparent hair hats need a number of round braces, but not so many as for a stretched frame. In a medium-sized brim braces one inch apart are sufficient. For an irregular-shaped brim the braces must outline the curves of the hat, or the braid will make an ugly line.

Edge wire for hair hats should be wrapped with maline. This gives a foundation to which the first row of braid may be sewn.

Wire-Frame Uses to Be Avoided

The following " don'ts " will be invaluable in making wire frames.

Never sew any except hair or transparent braid over a wire frame, as a wire frame braced sufficiently to hold braid will be heavier than a pressed frame, and wire headsizes are never so comfortable.

Never fit velvet over a wire frame, as the wires make a mark or mar on the velvet, which is ugly. The effect is never smooth. The headsize is never comfortable. The edge finish is always bulky.

Never try to use a factory (ready-made) wire frame for really fine use, for the wire is always a poor quality, the outline of the edge wire is bad, braces are used where there is no need for them, and are omitted where they are needed, and the crowns are of an ungainly shape. There are very few times when it is desirable to use a wire-crown foundation for a transparent hat.

II. MATHEMATICAL SIDE OF FRAME MAKING
Mathematical Principles Involved

Most girls feel that the time spent on geometry is wasted. Millinery is an outstanding example of the practical application of geometry. Certainly one may make a hat without having studied geometry, but a knowledge of circles, lines, and angles helps one immensely in frame construction and in cutting and fitting.

Theoretically, the back and front brace wires are one straight line forming the diameter of a circle, which is the edge-wire circumference. So, too, are the brace wires from side to side and from side front to side back.

In the illustration, Figure 1, wires GE

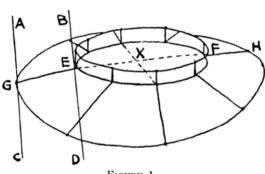

Figure 1.

WIRE FRAMES

and FH extended across the headsize of the frame (dotted line EF) make the diameter of the circle.

In frame construction, the same mathematical rules may be applied to a wire frame as to a circle. The edge wire is a circle with the center cut out for a headsize. Point X, the line of intersection, is the center of the circle. The braces form radii and diameters.

Mathematical Accuracy

Measures for wire frames must be absolutely exact if the hat is to be professional in appearance and becoming in line.

In a perfect frame a tangent drawn on the circle (the headsize and edge wires) at the point of intersection of the diameter (the brace wires) forms a right angle with the diameter. See lines BC and AD. That is, the brace wire must slant on a true right angle straight from the headsize to the edge. If it is slanted to either side of the perpendicular, the given measures will be wrong and the edge wire pulled out of shape.

Enlarging or Reducing Dimensions

Either of these processes can be performed without destroying the correct proportions.

In geometry the rule is that pi × the diameter of a circle equals the circumference. In a wire frame one brace wire equals a radius or two brace wires as line GH equals the diameter. So pi (3.14159$^+$) × 2 × the brace wire drawn from point X equals the edge wire.

The edge wire is always given by the designer when she shapes the frame. The puzzling part is to make the frame larger or smaller and have the edge wire so exact that the slant of the brim will not be lost.

1. **A larger edge wire.** If a frame is to be made $\frac{1}{2}$ inch larger all around, 1 inch is really added to the diameter, $\frac{1}{2}$ inch on each end of the diameter or each side of the hat — mathematically speaking, $\frac{1}{2}$ inch on each radius. So *pi*, or 3.1⁺, × 1 inch = the amount added to the circumference = 3.1⁺.

In the dimensions given for the hat in Figure 4 the edge wire is $44\frac{3}{8}$ inches. If the hat is made $\frac{1}{2}$ inch larger all around, the edge wire will be $44\frac{3}{8}$ inches + $3\frac{1}{10}^{+}$ = $47\frac{1}{2}$ inches ⁻. One-half inch will be added to each brace wire.

If a frame is to be made one inch larger, two inches are actually added to the diameter, one inch at each end.

Then *pi* (3.1⁺) × 2 inches = the amount added to the edge-wire circumference = 6.2 ⁺ inches.

For the hat in Figure 4 an added inch all around the edge wire will be $44\frac{3}{8}$ + 2 × $3\frac{1}{2}$ (*pi*) = $51\frac{3}{8}$ inches.

2. **Smaller edge wire.** To make a frame smaller is a matter of subtraction instead of addition. To make a frame $\frac{1}{2}$ inch smaller, subtract $\frac{1}{2}$ inch from each brace wire (1 inch on the diameter) and subtract *pi* × this difference (1 inch) in diameter from the edge-wire circumference.

3. **Larger headsize.** When the headsize must be larger and the edge wire is left the original size, the brace wires are changed. A headsize is also a circle and the rule of *pi* × the diameter still holds good.

In the case of the edge wire, the changed diameter or radius measure is given.

In the case of the headsize, the measure for the changed circumference is given: that is, the headsize needs to be a given amount, 1 inch or 2 inches larger. So the brace wires must be shortened.

The headsize is a circle within a circle and the rule is inverted

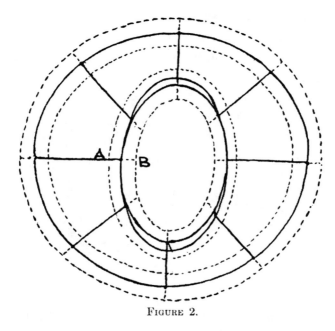

FIGURE 2.

(see Figure 2, headsize lines A extended to B). When a 25-inch headsize is to be made 1 inch larger (26 inches) the difference in the braces is the difference in circumferences or headsizes 1 inch $(26 - 25 = 1)$ $\div pi$ $(3.1\ ^+) = \tfrac{1}{3}$ inch $^+$. Each brace wire is made $\tfrac{1}{3}$ inch less.

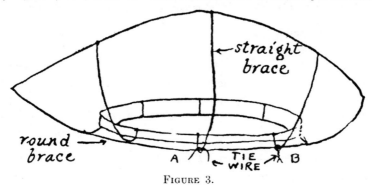

FIGURE 3.

4. Smaller headsize. When the headsize must be smaller the edge wire is left the original size; the brace wires must be longer to reach to the smaller inner circle (see Figure 2, lines A extended to B).

When a 25-inch headsize is to be made 1 inch smaller (24 inches) the difference in the braces is the difference in circumferences or headsize. 1 inch (25 − 24 equals 1 inch) ÷ pi (3.1$^+$) = $\frac{1}{3}$ inch$^+$. Each brace wire is made $\frac{1}{3}$ inch longer. The rule

FIGURE 4.

is the same as for making a headsize larger; but when the headsize is made smaller, length is added to the brace wire to make it reach the smaller inner circle.

III. PROCESS OF CONSTRUCTING A WIRE FRAME FOR HAT
(FIGURE 7)

CORRECT ORDER OF RECORDING MEASUREMENTS

Top headsize . . . . 24½ inches
Lower headsize . . . . 25 inches

Front	2¾ inches	Back	1⅛ inches
Left-side front	3⅜ inches	Right-side back	2½ inches
Left side	4¼ inches	Right side	4¼ inches
Left-side back	2½ inches	Right-side front . . .	3½ inches

Edge wire . . . . 44⅜ inches

The above order of recording measurements is used uniformly among good workmen. Note that the dimensions opposite each

WIRE FRAMES 11

other on a line are correspondingly opposite one another on a frame when assembled. Frames have usually eight braces. A frame with many curves, or one used for molding net and willow frames, may need more which can be added between the regular braces. Their length is gauged by the edge wire after it has been fastened to the regulation eight braces. Hence these extra braces rarely need measurement.

Getting Correct Headsize

Twenty-five inches is the average headsize for unbobbed hair. For bobbed hair twenty-two inches is the average size. To obtain a correct headsize measurement, pass a circle of wire around the head just where the headsize of a hat rests on the head. Allow $\frac{1}{8}$ inch for the space taken up by the underfacing of the hat and the headsize lining. Allow the circle to lap $2\frac{1}{2}$

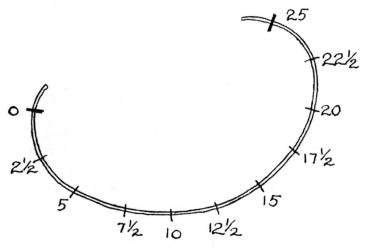

Figure 5 a. Marking the Headsize Wire.
Points 0 and 25 lap when the ends are tied to make the headsize oval.

inches and tie each end of the wire with a tie wire wrapped twice around and twisted tightly and cut. Make the upper of the two headsizes ½ inch smaller than the lower one, the lower being the one measured. To change headsize measurement see subdivision in this chapter on enlarging or reducing dimensions.

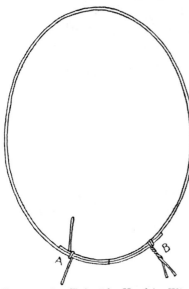

FIGURE 5 b. Tying the Headsize Wire.
Note that the tie wire is wrapped twice around the headsize wire and twisted before cutting off the ends.

GEOMETRICAL PRECISION REQUIRED

The following steps are to be taken with exactness.

1. **Marking the headsize for brace position.** Mark the headsize for the position of the brace wires, using a pencil on white wire and tailors' chalk on black wire. The first mark is for the back on the lap halfway between the two ends. Divide the headsize in eight sections starting with the tape measure at the back and marking *each* division as it is reached by the tape line.

Marking for a twenty-five-inch headsize. A twenty-five-inch headsize properly divided will be marked from the back as the starting point $3\frac{1}{8}$ — $6\frac{1}{4}$ — $9\frac{3}{8}$ — $12\frac{1}{2}$ (center front); $15\frac{5}{8}$ — $18\frac{3}{4}$ — $21\frac{7}{8}$ and 25 (the back). Lap the ends and tie each one to the headsize wire with a 1-inch length of tie wire.

The top headsize may be divided in the same way or only in four equal parts as the braces from the lower headsize will mark the one-eight divisions.

WIRE FRAMES   13

2. Mounting the brace wire.
To prepare the brace wire, cut eight brace wires 9 inches long and straighten them by running the cushion part (not the tip) of the thumb and forefinger slowly over the length of wire. When all curves have been thus removed, bend $2\frac{1}{2}$ inches from one end at right angles to the other. This bend B marks the position of the lower headsize wire. Place the lower (larger) headsize wire inside one of these wires at its center back, which was the first marked, and twist the brace wire around the back of the upper headsize about $\frac{3}{4}$ inch above the lower headsize wire and cut it off, leaving only a short end (about $\frac{1}{8}$ inch) to bend down. Next, put the front brace wire onto the two headsizes in the same manner, then right and left sides and side-front and side-back wires. To put the back wire on first insures firmness of the lapping, and the front second makes a true division and less confusion in working.

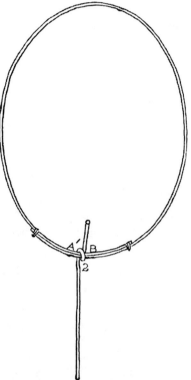

FIGURE 5 c. Placing the First Brace Wire.
Note the close wrapping around the headsize wire. The knot must be pinched close with the pliers, A to B, then pinched flat from 1 to 2.

3. Marking the brace wires for correct measurements. To mark the brace wires for correct measurements, place the zero end of the tape line at the lower base of the headsize. Measure to the given number and bend wire up at right angles.

14 MILLINERY

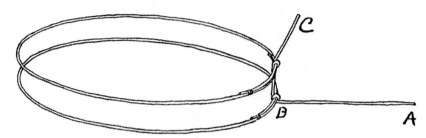

FIGURE 5 d.
Note the placement of the brace wire on the top and lower headsize wire.

Lap the back brace wire over the edge wire joining at the right angle and twist around once; cut off all but ⅛ inch end to bend down flat. Proceed with each brace wire in the same order as that used on the headsize.

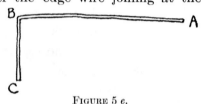

FIGURE 5 e.
Brace wire bent ready to put onto the headsize wires.

IV. DIMENSIONS FOR STANDARD HATS

The hat illustrated in Figure 6 gives the dimensions for a **medium-large mushroom** for lace.

MEDIUM ROLLED BRIM

Top headsize . . . . 24½ inches
Lower headsize . . . . 25 inches

Roll wire	1 inch	From headsize	29¾ inches
Front	3¼ inches	Back	3¼ inches
Left-side front	3¼ inches	Right-side back	3¼ inches
Left side	3¾ inches	Right side	3¾ inches
Left-side back	3¼ inches	Right-side front . . .	3⅛ inches

Edge wire . . . . 36 inches

WIRE FRAMES

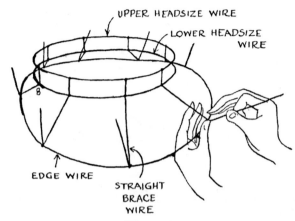

FIGURE 6.

Notice the closeness with which the brace wires are wrapped around the headsize and edge wires. The loop must be right before flattening it with the pliers. This means a quick, sharp bend of the brace wire close to the edge wire as is done in Figure 7.

Medium Small Poke

Top headsize	22 inches
Lower headsize	$22\frac{1}{2}$ inches

Front	$1\frac{3}{4}$ inches	Back	$1\frac{1}{2}$ inches
Left-side front	2 inches	Right-side back	$1\frac{5}{8}$ inches
Left side	$2\frac{1}{8}$ inches	Right side	$2\frac{1}{8}$ inches
Left-side back	$1\frac{5}{8}$ inches	Right-side front . . .	2 inches

Edge wire . . . . $27\frac{1}{4}$ inches

Child's Poke

Top headsize	$20\frac{1}{2}$ inches
Lower headsize	21 inches

Front	$1\frac{3}{4}$ inches	Back	1 inch
Left-side front	2 inches	Right-side back	$1\frac{1}{2}$ inches
Left side	$2\frac{1}{2}$ inches	Right side	$2\frac{1}{2}$ inches
Left-side back	$1\frac{1}{2}$ inches	Right-side front . . .	2 inches

Edge wire . . . . 30 inches

16　　　　　　　　　　MILLINERY

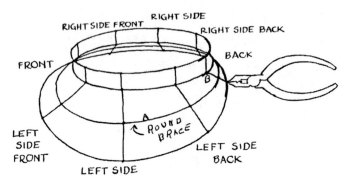

FIGURE 7.

Here is given the exact placement of the straight braces and the round brace wire used for some maline hats and for fitted flanges. Note the placement of the pliers in pinching the wire horizontally before flattening it vertically.

QUESTIONS

1. How is a knowledge of geometry of use in wire-frame making?
2. What are the two main uses of wire frames?
3. Give the wire-frame uses to be avoided.
4. How is the edge-wire measurement determined when the frame is to be made 1 inch smaller?
5. How is the edge-wire measurement determined when a brim is to be made $\frac{1}{2}$ inch larger?
6. What is the correct order of mounting the brace wires?
7. When are many round braces necessary?
8. How many round braces are needed for a transparent hat?

CHAPTER II

MOLDED FRAMES

I. MOLDED OR PRESSED FRAMES
   Process of manufacture
   Cost of manufacture
   Advantages of using a pressed frame
   Adjustment of pressed frame
   1. To adjust the headsize
   2. To make a mushroom from a sailor
   3. To make a poke from a mushroom
   4. To use a pattern on a pressed frame

II. HAND-MOLDED FRAMES
   Frames of various materials stretched on wire
   1. Willow
   2. Buckram
   3. Jockey
   4. Elastic net
   5. Rice net or cape net
   6. Crinoline
   Process of making a stretched frame
   1. Soaking frame fabric in water
   2. Pinning frame fabric to wire frame
   3. Drying frame fabric on the frame
   4. Removing frame fabric from the mold
   5. How to give variety to shapes stretched on the same frame
   6. How to wire a frame

III. BIAS DRY-MOLDED FRAMES
   When frames may be molded in this way
   Processes
   1. Frame molding in the hand
   2. Dry molding over a frame

QUESTIONS

I. MOLDED OR PRESSED FRAMES

Process of Manufacture

The original model for a pressed frame is a wire frame made by the designer (see Chapter I, section I). A model which is to be used for a manufacturer's mold must be a very firm frame closely braced, with any roll or bend perfectly outlined. For an irregular shape an extra, straight brace is usually added between each of the eight ordinarily used, making sixteen straight brace wires. The round braces should be about $\frac{1}{2}$ inch apart.

The wire model now goes to the molding room, where the block makers make a plaster cast or mold from it.

From the plaster cast a wooden mold is whittled or carved. This wooden block is kept in stock, as it may be used for shaping straw shapes as they are sewn by makers before sizing and blocking.

From the wooden block an hydraulic steel die is made. This consists of two forms, upper and lower, which fit together like an acorn in its cup.

In making the pressed frame buckram or net is soaked in water or a sizing solution and stretched over the heated lower steel die. The top half of the die is clamped down over it and left until the frame material is thoroughly dry. At least two men are required to operate this die, or press machine.

After the frame is pressed, the rough edges extending beyond the die must be trimmed, the headsize cut out, and the edge wired and bound by machine.

Cost of Manufacture

Pressed crowns are made in much the same way as brims. After all the expensive process of mold-making, two men are required to operate the machine on which the frames are pressed. On the average, the first frame made on an hydraulic die costs from $300 to $600. It may readily be seen that an enormous number of frames must be sold before the original cost is covered. In other words, the thousands of frames that must be sold from one die tend to make the shape a common one. Producers of exclusive millinery prefer to make hand-molded frames or to change the shape of the French frame in order to differentiate it.

ADVANTAGES OF USING A PRESSED FRAME

There are a number of advantages in using a pressed frame. Much expensive labor is saved. It takes almost as much time to prepare a hand-blocked frame as it takes to make the hat. The cost factor to the hat manufacturer is much less for a machine frame. The machine frame will stand more unskilled handling than a hand-molded frame. The pressed frame has a smoother and more finished appearance than a handmade frame.

To the uninitiated home milliner the hand-modeled frame often seems unfinished and imperfect. They see the rough-appearing surface rather than its beauty of line.

Pressed frames may be purchased from the millinery departments of the large department stores, from the better of the 50c and $1 stores, and from many of the mail-order houses.

ADJUSTMENT OF PRESSED FRAME

The average pressed shape should be purchased with the idea of changing it to suit the individual before using it.

1. To adjust the headsize. The headsize may be made larger by slashing the brim from headsize to edge and inserting a piece of buckram or elastic net. Rip the edge binding and the wire where it is lapped. Pin in the necessary piece of material. Try on the frame. Adjust the size. Bend the set-in piece at the headsize as the frame headsize is bent. Sew the seams firmly by machine or with a tight backstitch. Replace the edge wire with binding. To make the headsize smaller rip the binding and edge wire joining. Slash from edge to headsize and lap until the headsize fits. If the frame is a great deal too large, two slashes — one at the front and one at the back — are necessary. Too much lapping will throw the frame out of shape.

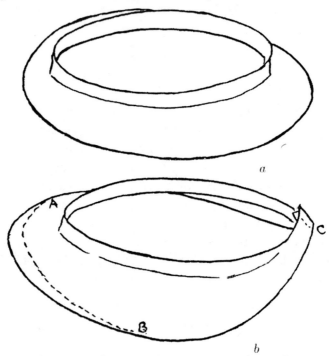

FIGURE 8. To Make a Poke Brim from a Mushroom Frame.

Illustration *a* is a plain mushroom brim from which a poke may be cut. In *b* note the lapped seam *C* and the dotted line *AB* for cutting the front.

2. **To make a mushroom from a sailor.** To make a mushroom from a straight sailor brim cut the brim at the back and front from edge wire to headsize, ripping the edge binding and edge wire. Make a seam which laps very little at the headsize, but a great deal more at the edge. Taking from the edge and not

from the headsize is what gives the mushroom effect. Trim some width of brim from the front and more from the back. The conventional mushroom needs to be proportionately narrower in front than a sailor, because when a frame droops it hides the face. A narrow back (see Figure 8) is always better because, first, a wide drooping effect makes thick-looking shoulders, and, second, because it interferes with comfort by knocking against coat collars, car windows, and seat backs.

3. **To make a poke from a mushroom.** This process is much the same as above, because the frame is already mushroom. Rip the binding and edge wire. Cut the back from edge to headsize. Slant the seam so that the edge laps from one to two inches and the headsize laps only ¼ inch.

4. **To use a pattern on a pressed frame.** Many of the mushroom-hat patterns may be cut from an ordinary pressed-sailor or mushroom frame. Cut off the headsize slashes of the pattern on the line marked "headsize." Pin the pattern onto the mushroom brim. Mark the correct edge and cut.

This does away with the necessity of wiring a headsize and with the bother of looking for correct frame material. The original edge binding may be replaced. Silk brace wire is more satisfactory for the edge wire. Poke patterns may be cut from mushroom frames in the same way. The important thing is to get the same slant and the same proportion as the hat pattern so that the same pattern may be used to cut the hat materials.

II. HAND-MOLDED FRAMES

Frames of Various Material Stretched on Wire

There are a number of frame materials that may satisfactorily be used for stretching frames. The ones most used are willow, buckram, jockey, elastic net, rice net, and crinoline.

Willow: See Chapter I, section I.
Buckram: See Chapter I, section I.
Jockey: See Chapter I, section I.
Elastic net: See Chapter I, section I.

Rice net is a frame material which is as much a net as wire window screening. A thread net held together by sizing (or starch) would properly define it. Cape net is the same thing with finer mesh. Rice net is used for stretching soft crowns and for small brims of very soft ribbon or braid sport hats. It makes a softer frame than elastic net. It is sometimes used with a thickness of crinoline.

Crinoline is used to stretch soft tam crowns, baby hats, old ladies' bonnets, and with rice net for larger hats. When crinoline and rice net are used together the two materials are stretched one over the other, pinned separately, but dried and removed together. The sizing sticks them together so that they hold nicely.

Process of Making a Stretched Frame

1. Soaking frame fabric in water. The first step in stretching a hand-molded frame is to soak the frame material to be used. Each of the fabrics mentioned under section II of this chapter has a great deal of sizing.

This needs only to be wet to become pliable. Then it may be stretched over any desired frame and it will dry in that shape.

2. Pinning frame fabric to the wire frame. Start pinning at the front on the edge wire. Use a bias corner of the willow. Pin to first one side of the brim, then to the other. Smooth the wet fabric over the wire frame, adding first a pin at the edge wire, then one at the headsize. Cut out a small headsize circle. Slash the material at the headsize to the lower headsize wire at intervals of $\frac{1}{2}$ inch. Do not slash below the lower headsize wire. Smooth all fullness out by pulling it out at the edge and headsize and pushing it backward to the seam.

Trim the headsize slashes, leaving only enough to pin over the top headsize wire.

Do not bend the material over the edge wire. Allow it to extend beyond the wire. Place pins at intervals of one inch.

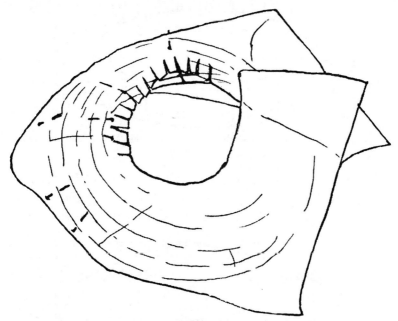

FIGURE 9. Pinning the Frame Fabric to the Wire Frame.

Be careful not to pull the frame too tightly between the straight brace wires, or the edge wire will lose its contour. There will be an angle on each straight brace at the edge wire.

3. Drying frame fabric on the frame. Hang the stretched frame up to dry above a hot radiator or in a window, if you want it to dry quickly. A good idea for class work is to stretch the frames in one lesson that are to be used for the next day. Then they may stand overnight. A frame must be thoroughly dried before it is removed from the wire mold.

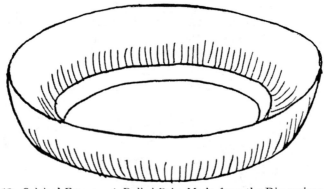

FIGURE 10. Original Frame. A Rolled Brim Made from the Dimensions Given in Chapter I, Section IV.

4. Removing fabric frame from the mold. When the frame is thoroughly dry, mark edge wire, headsize wire, and seam with a pencil. Pull out the pins from edge and headsize. Place them

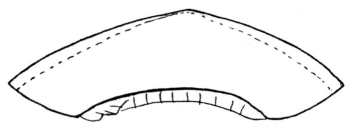

FIGURE 11. The Same Frame Made into a Tricorn.

in a separate box to be used for frames only. The starch on them will mark silk or velvet. Loosen the frame carefully at both edge and headsize. Remove a little at a time so as not to stretch it out of shape. Trim the back seam and lap it as it was marked if the headsize is the correct size. The headsize may be adjusted as for a pressed brim (see Chapter II, section I).

Cut headsize and wire edge at the pencil mark.

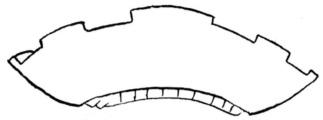

FIGURE 12. The Frame Made into a Square-Edge Tricorn.

5. How to give variety to shapes stretched on the same frame. If a wire mold has a good headsize roll as well as a becoming brim line, it may be changed in a variety of ways.

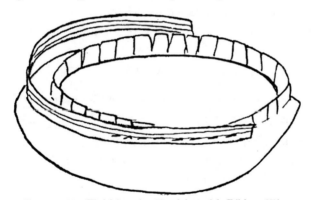

FIGURE 13. Finishing the Headsize with Ribbon Wire.

The brim may be merely cut smaller. It may be slashed at the side, or it may be cut to give an entirely different effect (see illustration, Figures 11 and 12).

6. To wire a frame. For the headsize, cut a half-inch bias band of dry frame material. Join this in a circle the same size as the brim headsize. Wire the lower headsize with brace wire, using a blanket stitch.

Lap the ends of the wire two inches.

Shape the circle of frame material and wire into an oval.

Slip this over the brim headsize with the unwired edge up.

Sew the oval to the slashes, using two rows of backstitching, one just above the wire and one at the top edge.

Straighten the wire for the edge by running the thumb and forefinger over it lengthwise, using the cushion part of the finger, not the tips. When the curve is thus worked out of the wire, buttonhole it to the top edge of the frame (edge-wire Figure 18), taking very tight stitches about three fourths of an inch long and only one sixteenth of an inch in from the edge. Lap the ends of the wire two and one-half inches and sew down firmly.

Bind the edge with a three-fourths-inch bias strip of muslin or flannel. Sew with long, tight, running stitches and stretch.

III. BIAS DRY-MOLDED FRAMES

When Frames May Be Molded This Way

If a frame turns up straight from the face instead of flaring out in a wide brim, there is less sewing in fitting the material. Often a bias may be stretched to fit it. A chinchin sailor, a rolled sailor, and many turbans may be stretched from a bias of elastic net, soft willow, or double crinoline.

If a frame can be stretched without wetting the material, the process is not only much shorter, because of the soaking and drying process eliminated, but it is much more tidy. The soaking method necessitates the use of many thicknesses of newspaper or rubber work-aprons to protect dresses from wet frame materials.

MOLDED FRAMES

Processes

1. Frame molding in the hand. There are wonderful possibilities for making rolled brims in the hand without a mold. Make a half-inch willow headsize band as for a stretched frame, or use a band of ribbon wire. Sew one edge of bias elastic net (the width determined by the height or width of the hat brim) inside the headsize. Curve the bias upward as you sew and crowd the material close to make it roll. Elastic net is preferable, but soft willow answers the purpose. If width at the sides is desired, or a point or decided angle anywhere, cut the bias and lap

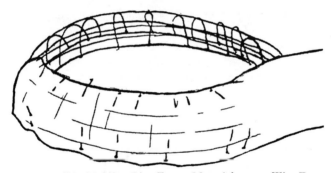

FIGURE 14. Dry Molding Bias-Frame Material over a Wire Frame.

it two or three inches at the headsize, allowing it to flare to a small seam at the edge.

2. Dry molding over a frame (see Figure 14). Bias net or willow may be stretched over wire molds without soaking, whenever the curve of the frame is such that there is no fullness left, or whenever the angle up from the face is very decided. Often this means more than one seam. The extra seams are usually on the brim angle. The stretching, removing, and wiring process is the same as for a wet frame (see section II, of this chapter).

QUESTIONS

1. How are original frame shapes made?
2. Name the processes involved in making the first buckram frame of a new design.
3. What is the greatest cost element?
4. How may a pressed-frame headsize be made larger?
5. How may a pressed-frame headsize be made smaller?
6. What advantages has a pressed ready-made frame for the home milliner?
7. Name the frame materials used for hand-stretched frames.
8. Give the detailed steps used in making a hand-stretched frame.
9. What is a dry-molded frame?
10. Make a dry-molded frame, doll-size. Copy the shape from a given drawing.
11. What are the important points in making a wire frame for stretching purposes?
12. Make two doll-size wire frames for models.

CHAPTER III

PATTERN FRAMES

I. CLASSIFICATION OF FRAMES MADE FROM PATTERNS
   Straight brims
      1. Mushroom
      2. Sailor
      3. Bias turban
   Rolled brims
      1. Thimbled rolls
      2. Headsize rolls
      3. Facing rolls
      4. Edge rolls
II. COMPARISON OF PROCESSES IN MAKING UNROLLED AND ROLLED BRIMS
III. CUTTING THE FRAME
   Placing of pattern
   Obtaining correct headsize
   Adjusting seams
   Importance of true-edge outlines
IV. WIRING FRAMES
   Different kinds of wire
      1. Brace wire
      2. Lace wire
      3. French wire
      4. Cable wire
      5. Ribbon wire
   Special uses of these wires
      1. Cable wire and French wire
      2. Lace wire
      3. French wire
      4. Cable wire
      5. Ribbon wire

Points of importance in wiring frames
Stitches used
   1. Blanket stitch
   2. Back stitch
V. BINDING A FRAME
VI. COVERING FRAME WITH INTERLINING
Kinds of interlining and their uses
   1. Fabrics
Stitches used
Effects to be obtained

QUESTIONS

I. CLASSIFICATION OF FRAMES MADE FROM PATTERNS

Since a pattern can represent only a flat surface, patterns can be made only for hats that have straight lines. The use of seams allows a frame to droop or to turn straight up from the headsize. A curved mushroom or an up-turned brim with an irregular curve must be stretched over a wire frame.

Any curves made in the shape of pattern brims are accomplished by thimbling or by the use of bias-frame material.

STRAIGHT BRIMS

Straight brims may be divided into three classes, mushroom, sailor, and bias turban brims.

1. Mushroom brims are brims that droop from the headsize down. The degree of droop, or mushroom, varies with the styles of the times and with the size of the hat.

The angle of the droop of a small mushroom brim may be much greater than that of a large brim. This is because a wide brim with a great deal of droop would entirely obscure the face.

2. Sailor brims are either perfectly straight flat brims or slightly mushroom. In either case a sprung steel wire is neces-

PATTERN FRAMES

sary for a large brim. This holds the edge firmly without springing out of shape.

3. Bias turban brims. A bias strip of elastic net or willow is often used to form the coronet of a turban. Usually such a frame has a headsize turn; that is, it is turned up at the headsize but not thimbled and has a flare at the brim edge. The measurements for headsize turn and the brim edge are given with the pattern (see Figure 15).

FIGURE 15.

ROLLED BRIMS

1. Thimbled rolls. All of the up-turned brims and brims with turned-up edges which are given in a pattern design have a roll that is made by thimbling (see Figure 16).

Thimbling a roll. To make the roll in a frame, hold the outside of the frame in the palm of the left hand and rub the inside with the thimble on the thimble finger of the right hand.

2. Headsize rolls are usually directly at the headsize so that the brim turns up from the face. Ordinarily an extra wire is not needed.

3. Facing rolls are often an inch or more from the headsize, in which case a wire is used and measurement is given for it.

Often rolls are at the back, others are at the front or side. An extra brace is seldom used except for very large brims.

4. Edge rolls. Edge rolls may be a very slight shaping of the frame or may be an extra bias strip added. In some cases this is a fold of elastic net added after the frame is wired.

In other cases a pencil roll is used. For this finish, the frame has a thick pencil-like roll on the edge. One edge of a bias strip

32   MILLINERY

is sewn to the wired edge of a brim. The other edge of the bias strip is rolled up over the top of the brim and wired with a circle of wire slightly larger than the brim edge wire. Measurements for this wire are always given on the pattern, as the roll varies from one inch to three inches.

II. COMPARISON OF PROCESSES IN MAKING UNROLLED AND ROLLED BRIMS

In making a straight unrolled brim the headsize is wired first, then the edge is wired.

In making a rolled brim the headsize is wired first, then the roll is thimbled and wired if necessary. The edge is wired last.

III. CUTTING THE FRAME

PLACING OF PATTERN

Always place the pattern so that the center front is at the bias corner of the material.

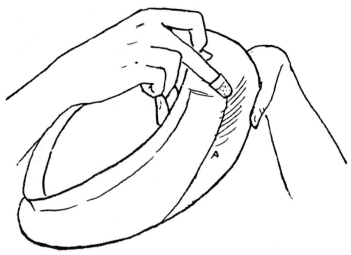

FIGURE 16. Thimbling a Frame.

PATTERN FRAMES 33

When willow is used, place the pattern on the frame material so that the rough side is the top of the frame. The cloth side is then on the under side.

When the headsize is slashed and the slashes bent up, the slashes are held up by the cloth and do not break off as they would if the smooth side were on top.

When the brim is rolled, the smooth cloth side of the willow holds the curve better than the fiber side.

Obtaining Correct Headsize

Measure a correct headsize by slipping frame wire around the head where the hat is worn. Hold the end of the wire firmly, so that the measured circle cannot slip. Allow two and one-half inches for lapping, and cut the wire. Tie the ends down with short lengths of tie wire, or wrap strong thread firmly over each end and sew through the silk wrapping of the wires.

Shape the wire circle thus formed into an ellipse and slip inside the frame above the slashes on the line marked " headsize wire." If the headsize is larger than the average, the wire will come below the line; if smaller, the headsize wire will come above the headsize line. Sew this wire to the headsize line with a blanket stitch (see Figure 19). Patterns are made the average headsize, which is 23 to 25 inches.

Figure 17. Hat Made on Ribbon Wire for the Frame.

Adjusting Seams

Frame seam allowances are always made on the patterns. To make a frame headsize smaller or larger, always make an extra seam in the front if there is a difference of more than ¾ inch desired in the headsize. To take more than ¾ inch out or to add more than ¾ inch at one place spoils the line of the hat.

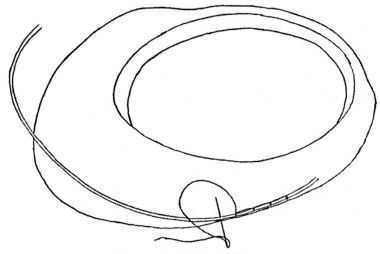

Figure 18. Wiring the Frame.

Importance of True-Edge Outlines

A true-edge outline is no mere matter of chance. It is a geometrical thing. The outline of a hat frame must be absolutely true in curve or angle. An angle is always decided- not accidental-looking.

An edge of a hat must be always one of two things; a perfect ellipse, or an ellipse with a definite irregularity added in a turned curve or a decided angle.

PATTERN FRAMES

Always trim an edge carefully before wiring it. Try to train the eye to see curves in absolutely correct perspective.

IV. WIRING FRAMES

Different Kinds of Wire

1. **Brace wire** is more commonly and widely used than any other one wire. For frame wiring, for wire frames, and for edge-wire finishes it is very satisfactory and especially so for student work (see Chapter V, section I).

2. **Lace wire** is used for wiring soft frames for sport hats, and for children's hats, and for lace bows and edges.

3. **French wire** is used for wiring frames and for edge wires. It makes a less stiff hat than brace wire does (see Chapter V, section I).

4. **Cable wire** is used for frames only when a thick-edge effect is desired.

5. **Ribbon wire** is used to wire frame edge when a fold effect is desired, and for headsize bands.

It is sometimes used as a cording over which fabric or ribbon is shirred. In such cases it forms the only frame used. Measurements and directions are given on the pattern for this type of hat (see Figure 17).

Special Uses of These Wires

1. **Cable wire** and **French wire** may be used for the same purposes. The former simply makes a firmer hat.

2. **Lace wire** is needed for wiring high lace ruffles and for lace or hair-braid edges and for lace flowers.

3. **French wire** is needed for frames and finished edges where soft effects are desired.

36 MILLINERY

4. **Cable wire** is used for only a few edges.

5. **Ribbon wire** is much used for soft, fold frame edges and for headsize-band finishes.

Points of Importance in Wiring Frames

The wire must always have the curve worked out before it is sewed to the frame. Straighten the wire by running the thumb and forefinger over it lengthwise, using the cushion part

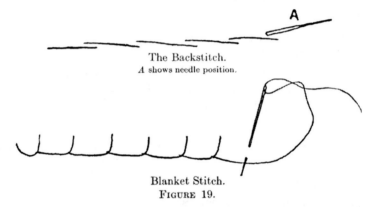

The Backstitch.
A shows needle position.

Blanket Stitch.
FIGURE 19.

of the thumb and finger, not the tip. If the tips of the thumb and finger are used, they bend the wire instead of straightening it.

The wire must be sewn at the edge above or below. It cannot be directly on the edge. There is nothing to hold it, and the wire slips.

Stitches Used

1. A **blanket stitch** is used for sewing the headsize wire to the frame, for wiring the edge of a brim, and for sewing on the wire at a roll. For this the needle must be stuck through the frame and pushed back to catch the thread knot (see figures 18 and 19).

2. A **backstitch** is used for sewing a headsize band to the slashes of the headsize (see Figure 19, *A*).

V. BINDING A FRAME

In binding a frame edge, bias crinoline is used for a flat edge (see Chapter VI, section IX). The crinoline should be stretched lengthwise and sewed flat on the frame with running stitches half an inch long.

Always have the binding about an inch wide after stretching. Sew the binding at its edge. The object is to protect the hat

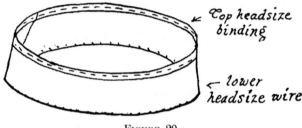

FIGURE 20.

covering from being marred or worn by the edge wire. A binding should be sewn so as to blur the wire, not emphasize it.

VI. COVERING FRAME WITH INTERLINING

An interlining is needed to keep the frame from showing through straw braid or fabric and to give an appearance of softness to a hat. Satin without an interlining makes a hard-looking hat.

KINDS OF INTERLINING AND THEIR USES

The **fabrics** most used for interlinings are cotton flannel, mull, and silkoline.

Cotton flannel is soft, thick, and lightweight. It is preferable except when a thin fabric is used for the hat, and a matching color in interlining is needed.

For colored georgette, lightweight colored crêpes, and thin, dark-colored satin or messaline, *mull*, or *silkoline* in matching shades is used for interlinings.

Thin black satin or messaline needs a *self-colored interlining* only, because the white interlining shows at the needle points in the edge-wire finish.

For very light-colored georgette, as flesh, primrose, or orchid, *white cotton flannel* is preferable to a thinner material of a self color because it gives a more spongy, soft effect to the crêpe. A thin, closely woven interlining often gives crêpe a hard surface.

Stitches Used

As a general rule the same stitches are used for an interlining as for the outer fabric. A frame is covered as though silk or velvet were used.

In covering a frame with interlining for a braid hat, the edge stitches need not be carefully done because the braid hides them.

An interlining for a fabric underfacing is sewn separately at the headsize, but interlining and facing are turned over the facing wire together. If they are turned separately, the crêpe or silk edge shows in an ugly edge outline. The facing and the wire are apt to show through the fabric.

Effects to Be Obtained

The effects desired in the use of interlinings are to soften the hat effect, and to keep the frame from showing through the straw braid or fabric.

Interlining can never be close, heavy material, or it will tend to make a heavy hat.

The quality of lightness in a hat is just as important as beauty and becomingness are.

QUESTIONS

1. What three kinds of frames come under the classification of straight frames?
2. Give directions for thimbling a roll.
3. What is a pencil roll? How is the frame made for a hat with a pencil roll?
4. What is the difference in the process of wiring a straight frame; a roll frame?
5. Give directions for placing a pattern on frame material; for placing a pattern on willow.
6. How is a correct headsize obtained?
7. Name the kinds of wire used for wiring frames.
8. When is ribbon wire used for a frame?
9. What stitches are used in wiring a frame?
10. Give directions for binding a frame.
11. What kind of interlining is used for georgette crêpe: in black; in flesh; why?
12. What kind of interlining is used for a dark shade of thin satin? Why?
13. What, geometrically speaking, is a hat outline?

CHAPTER IV
CROWNS

I. FRAME FOUNDATIONS USED FOR CROWNS
   Pressed crowns
       1. Desirable kinds of pressed crowns
   Side crown foundations
II. KINDS OF CROWNS
   Cap crowns
       1. Plain oval-top crown
       2. Small oval-side crown shirred on cord
       3. Round top crown
       4. Method of mounting
       5. Seam placement
   Plain sectional
       1. Kinds of sectional crowns
       2. Method of assembling sectional crowns
   Section cap crown with draped side crown
       1. Assembling
       2. Mounting the top crown
       3. Draping the side crown
   Tam crowns
       1. Fitted or circular crowns
       2. Sectional tams
       3. Saddle tams
       4. Round tam with bias sides
   Fitted crowns
       1. Fitted or pressed crowns
       2. Draped side crown
       3. Fitted top crowns
       4. Sectional crowns fitted on pressed crowns

Soft semifitted crowns
    1. Draped
    2. Sectional
III. OUTLINE OF KINDS OF CROWNS AND THEIR APPROPRIATE BRIMS
IV. HOW TO DETERMINE KINDS OF CROWNS SUITABLE TO INDIVIDUAL TYPES OF FACES
What decides the kind of crown to be worn
Rules for choosing crowns
    1. For the wide face oval
    2. For the narrower face
    3. For the long, thin face
    4. For the short face oval

QUESTIONS

I. FRAME FOUNDATIONS USED FOR CROWNS

PRESSED CROWNS

A pressed crown is the simplest foundation to use for a crown because it may be purchased ready for use. When a soft crown is desired, the top of the crown may be cut out with a razor blade after the hat is completed but before the hat is lined.

1. Desirable kinds of pressed crowns. A soft pressed crown (one made of elastic net, crinoline, or very lightweight jockey buckram) is always the most satisfactory, both from the point of view of comfort and of appearance.

Plain oval. A plain oval crown is the best foundation for most cap and section crowns.

Cuff crowns. An oval pressed crown with plain or draped separate cuff around the side crown may be used for mounting a cap crown (see section II, of this chapter), and for mounting a fitted cap with a draped side (see section II, of this chapter).

Shaped oval crowns. Shaped oval crowns — for example, one that is larger at the top and higher on the left side — often make good frames (or molds) over which to sew braid crowns. (See Chapter VIII, section II.)

SIDE CROWN FOUNDATIONS

A bias strip of elastic net or willow may be cut to fit the brim headsize; the width of this band varies from 2 to 4 inches according to the kind of crown. Start with 4 inches and cut it lower if desired. Stretch the bias frame material so that the headsize is larger around than the top of the band. After it is shaped trim the headsize edge and wire and bind it.

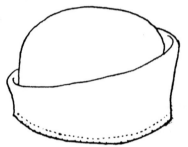

FIGURE 21. Pressed Crown with Cuff Side Crown.

Cut the top edge so that it slants down in a lower curve on the right side. Bind it as for a frame edge.

II. KINDS OF CROWNS

CAP CROWNS

A cap crown is a soft crown made with an oval or round top and a bias side.

1. Plain oval-top crowns. The most commonly used cap crown has an oval top and a bias side which measures from 5 to 8 inches. The variation of width depends on the amount of drape desired in the side crown.

The oval top may be used in two ways.

Long from front to back. The plain oval-top crown may be placed so that it is long from front to back, with the folds draped a little deeper on the right side.

Wide from side to side. The plain oval-top crown may be used so that its length is from side to side. The folds of the drape are then deeper at the sides, because the oval brings the side crown down lower at the sides, so that the crown stands higher in front and back than at the sides. The cap may be pushed back on the pressed crown so that the front is much higher than the back. This draping of a cap crown is becoming to a woman with a wide face oval (see section III of this chapter).

2. **Small oval-side crown shirred on cord.** This is often used on a hat for a girl who has a small face. The top crown is so small that it is not much more than a tip. It varies in size from an oval of $4\frac{1}{2}$ by 3 inches to an oval of 3 by $2\frac{1}{4}$ inches.

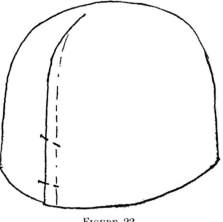

FIGURE 22.

3. **Round top crown.** Occasionally a round top, a perfect circle, is used for a cap crown, usually in a semidraped soft hat.

4. **Method of mounting.** Since a cap crown should always be soft in appearance it is usually mounted on a soft pressed crown or a bias side band of elastic net.

5. **Seam placement.** The seam in the side of a cap crown should always be placed where it shows least.

In an even drape place the bias seam so that it starts at the center back and runs toward the right side. It will be less conspicuous on the right side. The hat is worn tilted down on the right side. Any trimming is usually on the right side.

In an uneven drape the seam should always be placed where the side crown is lowest and the seam shows least.

44   MILLINERY

When there is a side-crown trimming, the seam of the bias side may be placed so that the trimming covers it.

Plain Sectional

Plain sectional crowns are semifitted soft crowns made of a number of pie- or wedge-shaped sections.

1. Kinds of sectional crowns. The various kinds of sectional crowns are: two-section crowns, four-section crowns, six-section crowns, eight-section crowns.

2. Method of assembling sectional crowns. (Exact directions are always given on each section-crown pattern.)

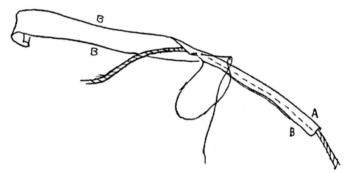

FIGURE 23. An Unfinished Cord.

Plain sectional crowns. The method is always to baste from the center top down to the headsize before stitching. If the material used is very soft or very lightweight, an interlining is used. Care is needed to keep the seam smooth but not stretched.

Corded sectional crown — an unfinished bias cord is used to outline the sections (see Figure 23).

For an even number of sections — there are two methods of cording (see figures 24 and 25).

Cording half the sections is a method used when only half the sections are outlined with cord from the headsize to the center and down to the headsize again.

They are then assembled with a plain section alternating with a corded one. This makes one cord on each seam and each cord pointed in a V at the center top crown.

Making a straight cord from front to back — in this method one length of cord is run from front to back of the crown. One

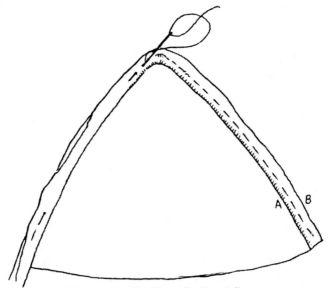

FIGURE 24. Cording a Sectional Crown.

section is sewn on each side of this cord with the central points meeting. Any extra sections are then outlined with cord (from headsize to center and from the top to the headsize) and set in.

In case of a four-section crown only one extra cord on each side is set in from headsize to center top.

For an uneven number of sections, the best method is to outline one side of each section with cord and let all cord ends meet at the center top. The ends are hidden on the seam side. It will be seen that a fine soft cord is essential.

SECTIONAL CAP CROWN WITH DRAPED SIDE CROWN

The top of the crown is made of pie-shaped sections which form a circle or an oval.

1. Assembling. In this type of crown the top crown is assembled with or without cords as for a plain sectional crown.

2. Mounting the top crown. The circle edge of the section cap thus formed is shirred and the cap is mounted on a pressed crown, the fullness evenly distributed, and the cap sewn to the pressed crown.

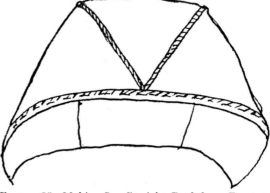

FIGURE 25. Making One Straight Cord from Front to Back in a Six-Sectional Crown.

3. Draping the side crown. The side crown is a bias strip fitted loosely and joined in a seam.

Seam placement. The seam is placed as for a cap crown (see section II, 5, of this chapter).

Draping. The side crown is draped in folds around the headsize. The width varies from 4 to 6 inches according to the fullness desired.

Finish. Top Edge. The top edge may be finished in two ways:

a. Fold finish. The edge may be turned in a fold and the fold slip-stitched to the cap.

b. Wire finish. The top edge may be turned over a wire, or corded and finished as for a flange edge (see Chapter VII, section II, under Fitted Hats).

Lower or Headsize Edge. The lower or headsize edge may be finished in any one of three ways:

a. Inside-the-crown finish. The edge may be turned up inside the crown and whip-stitched to the frame. This gives a fold finish.

b. Brim-fold finish. The headsize edge of the pressed crown may be sewn to the finished brim of the hat and the lower headsize edge of the side-crown drape pulled down over the crown headsize and slip-stitched to the brim.

c. Crown-wire finish. The headsize edge of the pressed crown may be bound with hat material and the bias side-crown drape may be worked over a wire and finished in the same way as the top edge is finished (see section II of this chapter).

Tam Crowns

Tam crowns are larger than other crowns and are always soft and loose. The drape should be adjusted after the hat is complete so that the lines are becoming to the type of individual.

They are all cut by patterns where seam placement and mounting directions are given.

1. **Fitted** or **circular crowns** are crowns with round or oval tops and a side crown which is cut from a segment of a large circle edge.

2. **Sectional tams** are larger but are treated much the same as plain sectional crowns. The shapes are different in outline because the extra flare is fitted into the same headsize as any other crown. The assembling of the sections is just the same (see section II of this chapter). See Figure 33, page 80.

Six-section.
Four-section.
Eight-section.
Five-section.

3. Saddle tams. Saddle tams are shaped with a long fitted strip running from side to side and with circular-shaped sections at front and back. See Figure 35, page 81.

Directions for assembling are always given in the patterns.

4. Round tam with bias side. In making this kind of tam the bias is held a little full to give extra flare, but never enough to make shirrings at the top-crown seam.

Fitted Crowns

Fitted crowns differ from other kinds in that the different pieces are fitted and sewn separately to the pressed crown.

1. Fitted or pressed crowns. A top piece is fitted and sewn or pasted onto the top of a pressed crown, and a plain bias side crown fitted and finished with a fold or a wire finish (see section II of this chapter).

2. Draped side crown. This variety is the same as 1, but has a wider bias side. The extra width is draped in folds around the side crown. Many of the pressed crowns now on the market have plain or folded cuff sides over which the draped side crown may be folded.

Place the bias side-crown seam where it will show least.

3. Fitted top crowns. Fitted top crowns may have a bias side crown which is corded in groups of three or more or which is corded at regular spaces.

4. Sectional crowns fitted on pressed crowns. A sectional crown (see section II, page 42 of this lesson) may be assembled and fitted over a pressed crown.

Soft Semifitted Crowns

1. Draped. Under this heading come the crowns that are draped with the extra fullness cut out. Folds are laid to match on the cut edges and an unfinished cord set in.

2. Sectional. A bias piece is fitted around a pressed crown. The lower edge is finished plain or draped in a fold. The top edge is cut in pie with a section pattern and the seams stitched plain or corded.

IV. HOW TO DETERMINE KINDS OF CROWNS SUITABLE TO INDIVIDUAL TYPES OF FACES

What Decides the Kind of Crown to Be Worn

The contour of the face — the proportion of the face oval — always determines the kind of crown suitable to the individual. The crown of the hat makes the complemental (top half) of the oval.

Rules for Choosing Crowns

1. For the wide face oval. The crown must never be narrower than the face at its widest point. A narrower crown makes a wide face seem wider in proportion.

Wide, soft crowns are most becoming to wide faces. Four-section tams, round tams, saddle crowns, or cap crowns wide from side to side are good types.

2. For the narrower face. The fitted crown must never be wider than the face oval at its widest point. A crown too wide overshadows a narrow face until the face seems even smaller.

A soft drape may be used without spoiling the proportion.

A soft, not too-wide crown is best for a narrow face, as cap crowns and soft six- and eight-section crowns.

3. For the long, thin face. The long, thin face must have a comparatively low, not too wide, crown. A very high or stiff crown must never be chosen. It adds and exaggerates length.

III. OUTLINE OF KINDS OF CROWNS AND THEIR APPROPRIATE BRIMS

	Oval Cap Crown, Long from Front to Back. Chapter IV. sec. 11.	Oval Cap Crown, Wide from Side to Side. Chapter IV. sec. 11.	2-Section Crowns. Chapter IV. sec. 11.	4-, 6-, and 8-Section Crowns. Chapter IV. sec. 11.	Circular Tam Crowns. Chapter IV. sec. 11.	Sectional Tam Crowns. Chapter IV. sec. 11.	Saddle-Tam Crowns. Chapter IV. sec. 11.	Fitted Crowns. Chapter IV. sec. 11.	Sectional Fitted Crowns. Chapter IV. sec. 11.	Soft Fitted Crowns. Chapter IV. sec. 11.
Medium-large Sailor Brim		★	★		★	★				★
Small Sailor Brim	★		★							★
Large Mushroom Brim		★	★		★					★
Medium Mushroom Brim	★	★	★	★						★
Small Mushroom Brim	★	★	★	★	★					
Large Poke Brim			★	★	★					
Medium Poke Brim		★	★	★	★	★				★
Small Poke Wide from Side to Side		★		★	★					
Small Poke Long Front	★			★				★		
Medium-large Tricorn Brim	★			★				★	★	
Small Tricorn Brim	★			★					★	
Large Irregular Brim	★	★		★		★				★
Small Irregular Brim	★			★				★		
Medium-large Rolled Brim	★	★				★		★	★	
Small Rolled Brim	★			★				★	★	★

CROWNS

A very flat crown is out of proportion and makes for exaggeration.

Soft crowns of medium height and width complement the long, thin face. Soft cap crowns, long from front to back, section cap crowns, and circle cap crowns are very good for this type.

4. For the short face oval. The short face oval must avoid extremely high crowns and extremely wide crowns. A very high crown makes the face seem shorter by contrast. A very wide crown looks heavy and adds to the apparent width of the face.

Medium-high crowns with soft, irregular width are best for this class, as soft crowns wide from side to side and two-section crowns.

QUESTIONS

1. Define a cap crown, a section crown, a tam crown, a sectional cap crown.
2. What is the important point in seam placement?
3. Give two ways of assembling a corded sectional crown which has an even number of sections.
4. What principle decides the kind of crown to be worn by any individual?
5. Name the kinds of crowns becoming to four distinct types of individuals.
6. Make five different kinds of crowns, doll-size.
7. Give two kinds of crowns that may be used with each of five distinct types of hats as given in the Outline, section IV.

CHAPTER V

STAPLE MILLINERY MATERIALS

I. MATERIALS USED
  Fabrics
    1. Velvets
    2. Silks
    3. Cotton and linen fabrics
    4. Laces
    5. Straw cloths
  Braids
    1. Tests for quality
    2. Varieties
  Body
    1. Process of manufacture
    2. Tests of quality
    3. Varieties
  Trimmings
    1. Tests of quality
    2. Varieties
  Frames
    1. Process of manufacture
    2. Varieties
  Findings
    1. Covering
    2. Wire
    3. Threads
    4. Liquid preparations
    5. Needles

QUESTIONS

STAPLE MILLINERY MATERIALS

I. MATERIALS USED

The definitions and tests given in this lesson apply to millinery fabrics only. The qualities desirable for hat fabrics, such as velvet or satin, are very different from the qualities desired in the same fabrics when they are to be used for dresses. Hat materials must be nicely finished; the velvet pile, deep; the satin, lustrous. They must be light in weight. They need have no enduring wearing qualities. There is no strain on hat materials as there is on material for other wearing apparel.

FABRICS

1. Velvets.

Process of manufacture. Velvet is a soft, thick fabric with a deep silk pile. The warp is woven on a cotton woof. In a very expensive quality there is a silk back, or woof.

In weaving the warp the silk is passed over fine wires in such a way as to form rows of loops which project from the cotton back. When the wires are withdrawn there is left a fine, soft, silk pile.

In uncut velvet these loops are left intact.

For most millinery velvet the loops are cut with a sharp tool to make what is called cut velvet.

The best quality of millinery velvet is silk Lyons. The name is derived from the city of Lyons, in France, where much of it is made. For this, first-grade silk stock, called the first spinning, is used.

The trade of velvet weaving is a closed trade handed down from father to son. Velvet manufacturers say that "a velvet loom improves with usage. It takes one hundred years to perfect one of the looms for the finest weaving." During the World War many of these looms were allowed to rust and ruin.

For cheaper velvets, called chap velvets, the second spinning is used. For this second grade of silk velvet, the knots, ravelings, and ends of silk left from the first spinning are boiled and dissolved in a prepared solution and respun. A cheaper grade of cotton woof is used than for the Lyons velvet.

Tests of quality. Millinery velvet must have a close, soft nap which does not allow the woof, or back, to show through. It must be very light in weight but have body which holds it up. It should be silky in effect, showing light and shadow in such a way as to give an appearance of depth to black velvets and an effect of many shades of the same color to colored velvets. This effect is the result of the play of light on the deep silk pile.

Varieties. The varieties used for millinery are the only ones given.

Silk Lyons velvet is used for fitted and draped hats, both large and small. It is also used for handmade flowers and appliqué embroidery.

Chiffon or *uncut velvet* is really a dress fabric but is occasionally used for draped hats and often used for children's hats.

Chap velvet is used for less expensive hats. It has a higher lustre than Lyons velvet and is used for juniors' and children's hats.

Soleil or *panne* is Lyons velvet which is mirrored, or panned, by machine on the bias. To mirror on the bias gives a different gloss than to mirror on the straight of the material.

Paon velvet is chap velvet which has been mirrored on the straight. It has a high lustre but is a cheaper and a heavier-weight material than soleil.

Plush is woven of silk and wool. The weave is the same as for velvet. Only very lightweight plushes can be used for hats. Usually satin or taffeta is used in combination to keep the hat from being heavy or thick-looking.

2. Silks.

Tests of quality. Tests of quality for silks in millinery are the same as those for dress silks. None of the very thin grades of silks and satins is good. Messaline satin or thin taffeta, for example, are not fit to use because they draw needle slits wherever a stitch is taken on a frame. Even with an interlining it is impossible to make a nice hat from them.

Varieties of silks. There are, nevertheless, a number of silks that can be used.

Crêpes. Crêpe is a silk fabric woven with a spongy surface. Raw silk or a silk and wool mixture is used for the weaving.

Georgette is a very thin crêpe of silk and wool. The texture, though thin, is very strong. It is used for summer hats, for transparent hats, for children's hats, for facings in straw and velvet hats, and for handmade flowers. Folds of georgette are used in embroidery designs.

Canton crêpe is a very heavy crêpe with a rough surface. It is used for summer and mid-season hats and for facings in velvet hats.

Crêpe de chine is a medium-weight, dull crêpe used for summer hats, for children's hats, and for facings in straw and velvet hats. For all-over-embroidery hats crêpe de chine makes a good foundation.

Taffeta is used for early spring hats, for combination with straw braids, and for facings in straw and velvet hats.

Satin should always have a high lustre for millinery use. It is used for fall and midwinter hats and in combination with velvet and straw, both as a drape and for facings.

Chiffon is a silk gauze-like material used for transparent hats and for shirred children's hats.

3. Cotton and linen fabrics.

Tests of quality are the same as for dress goods of the same type.

Varieties used for hats are many. Only the chief ones are listed.

Organdies, plain and embroidered, are used for lingerie and sport hats and for handmade flowers.

Linens, plain, figured, and embroidered, are used only for sport hats. The colors and textures are very lovely and lend themselves to fancy appliqué and stitchings.

Cretonnes, in figured designs in both cotton and linen, are used for sport and lingerie hats.

4. **Laces.**

Tests of quality may be limited to appearance. A tinsel lace must not have cotton threads and must not be too heavy. Black laces should be silk, as cotton fades to a dull green in the sun.

Varieties. There are three kinds of laces used in making hats.

Silk laces are used in black for transparent dress hats and for trimmings. Écru silk laces are used for lingerie dress hats.

Cotton laces are used in écru or in tints for trimmings on children's hats and for lingerie hats.

Tinsel laces are used in winter for making dress hats in transparent models, for draped turbans, and for cut-out appliqués on fabric hats.

5. **Straw cloths.** Straw cloths are made of various compositions, made to look like straw. *Candy cloth, visca cloth,* and *hair cloth* are the ones in greatest usage.

BRAIDS

1. **Tests for quality.** The tests for quality for braids are mainly those of appropriateness, of beauty, and of weight. For dress hats, smooth braids with a high lustre are most effective. Beauty of color and texture in braid always makes for a better looking hat. Weight is always a problem to be considered. A braid loosely

woven needs an interlining, so it must not be both loose and heavy.

2. **Varieties.** The braids used in millinery are of many kinds.

Chenille braid is a soft woolen braid woven in a variety of colors. It comes in lovely shades and is used for sport hats and for embroidery.

Yarn braids are used entirely for sport hats. Crowns at least may be sewn without a foundation.

Visca braid comes under the class of straw braids, but is really a composition. It has a high lustrous finish and is appropriate for both dress and street hats.

Celophane braid is made of a celluloid composition. It has much the same finish as patent leather and is used for dress and street hats. A combination of hair braid and celophane braid is very effective.

Hemp braid is woven from hemp straw and is used for sport and street hats and for facings in summer fabric hats. It comes in fine stripping $\frac{1}{4}$ to $\frac{1}{16}$ inch wide. This is used for machine-sewn hats and for embroidery. When used for hand-sewn hats the stripping is machine stitched in rows to form a braid of $\frac{3}{4}$ to $\frac{7}{8}$ inch wide. It is then sewn by hand as any other braid is sewn.

Lisère braid is woven of fine wheat straw. It comes in stripping which is very narrow. This is sewn by machine for pressed-hat work. For hand-sewn hats the stripping is sewn up by machine to make a braid $\frac{1}{2}$ to $\frac{3}{4}$ inch wide. The finer qualities are very narrow.

Milan braid is woven from fine wheat straw. It derives its name from the city of Milan where it is extensively manufactured. It is used in the same way as hemp and lisère. See paragraphs above.

Hair is a transparent braid woven from a composition.

There are three qualities: (1) Swiss hair, the best quality; (2) German, a medium grade; and (3) domestic, a very inferior quality. The better grade has a fine hair, a good lustre, and body. The cheaper braids are shiny, sleazy, and have not much body.

Hair braid is used for transparent hats in summer and for combination with silk and taffeta on early spring hats. The latter are made on pressed frames.

Body Hats

Body hats are hats that have brim and crown woven in one.

1. Process of manufacture. The process of manufacture varies with the kind of hat. Most of the better straws, such as panamas, leghorns, and tuscan straws, are hand-woven by native workers. Felts are made almost entirely by machinery, as are sewed bodies.

2. Tests of quality. *Straw bodies* vary in quality with the fineness of the straw used and with the expertness of the weaver.

Among *felts*, the better grades are fine and close and need little sizing. The cheaper felts are loose and coarse. A great deal of sizing is used to give them body.

3. Varieties. *Felts* are made of a wool or wool and cotton composition, which is subjected to beating, heating, and pressure processes. The felt composition is rolled out into sheets. Body hats are blocked from sheets of felt with specially made steel machines. Felt manufactures form extensive industries in France, Switzerland, Germany, and Belgium. The finest felts are made in France and Switzerland.

Beaver and *velour* hats are made of felts which use the fur of rabbit, beaver, and raccoon in their composition. For beaver finish fine furs are drawn through the felt by an electric process.

The finest grade of velours and felts is made in Switzerland.

STAPLE MILLINERY MATERIALS

Leghorn hats are woven by hand in Leghorn, Italy. A very fine, bearded-wheat straw is used. The town gives the hat its name. Straw weaving is the principal industry. The finer the straw and the smoother the weaving, the better the grade of hat. Children start with coarse weaving and work up to the better grade as they grow older. The straw is woven into braid strips and these are woven into hats.

Tuscan is a very finely woven, golden, natural-straw-colored braid, usually made in lace-like patterns. It is sometimes woven into body hats and sometimes into braids which are sewn into body hats.

Panama hats are woven by natives of Panama, China, Japan, Cuba, and many of the southern islands. A fine grass is used. The weaving is done under water. Women's hats are sized and pressed into various shapes. They are used mainly for sport hats.

Sewed bodies are straw braids sewed by machine to form soft hats mainly used for sport wear. Hemp braid is sewn with angora yarn or visca straw outlining the seams. Yarn braids are sewn with silk strips or folds. Felt is cut with a pinking machine and sewn like a braid. Silk folds are sewn up into soft body hats on a box machine which gives the effect of handwork. They make lovely sport hats.

TRIMMINGS

1. Tests of quality. Tests of quality vary with the trimming. Finish, shape, fabric, quality, and good construction are the most important points. Where special points are important, they are given with the article.

2. Varieties. *Feathers* may be roughly divided into two classes:

a. Those used in their natural state. Ostrich, pheasant, many quills, and aigrettes are dyed but are often used without further change. The plumage of the male ostrich is of better quality than that of the female. The feathers of the male have larger, longer, and more glossy fiber.

b. Those made into fancies. Under this head come feathers that are mounted into wing shapes, and bird and fowl feathers that are glycerined, dyed, and mounted in fancy shapes and bands, such as peacock, ostrich, and goose.

Flowers. The best flowers are made of linen, fine satin, silk, and velvet.

Cheaper flowers are made from coarse cotton. Careful attention should be given to the color effects and glue construction, when choosing flowers.

Embroideries. Chinese and much peasant embroidery come already made and ready to be appliquéd on fabric and straw-cloth hats. Many fabric and cloth hats are trimmed with hand embroidery.

Ribbons. Ribbons are measured by the number of lignes in their width. For example, No. 9 ribbon has nine lignes, No. 12 has twelve lignes. Ribbon is used for tailored trimming, for binding, for finishes, and for handmade flowers and embroidery.

The varieties are grosgrain, satin, cire, tinsel, taffeta, silk fiber, and velvet. Each variety has hundreds of variations and patterns.

Ornaments. Ornaments come in many different shapes and forms. They are made of metal, celluloid, composition, glass, jet, and straw. They are used mainly on tailored hats and draped dress hats.

Pins. Pins are made of pearl, brass, gold, jade, platinum, rhinestone, jet, and glass. They are used on many different hats, usually as a finish.

STAPLE MILLINERY MATERIALS

Handwork. Handwork trims many street and dress hats. Under this heading come embroidery, braiding, beading, ribbon work, appliqué, and cutwork.

FRAMES

See Frames, Chapters I, II, and III.

1. Process of manufacture. See Frames, Chapters I, II, and III.

2. Varieties. The varieties used are *wire, willow, net,* and *buckram.*

FINDINGS

1. Covering. Covering or interlining is used under many satins, crêpes, silks, and straws.

Mull is a lightweight cotton material with a close weave and smooth finish.

Crinoline is used as an interlining where body is desired. It is also cut on the bias and used for frame bindings.

Cotton flannel is the best interlining for fabric hats and soft fabric crowns. It gives a much softer finish to the hat than a thinner covering.

2. Wire.

Steel wire is a heavy, sprung-steel wire covered or uncovered, which is used for edge wires on sailor brims or mushroom brims. It comes both in a round and square finish.

Cable wire is a fine steel wire covered with a padding and silk wrapping. It is used mainly for trimming braces and in machine work.

Brace wire is more used than any other one wire. It is a silk-wrapped, medium-fine wire which is very firm. It is used for wiring frames and for facing edges.

French wire is much like brace wire but is finer and not so stiff. It is largely used for wire-edge finishes and for many soft hats.

Lace wire is a very fine, silk-wrapped wire used for wiring lace, ribbon bows, and for very soft sport and children's hats.

Wire joiners are tiny steel cylinders used for joining the ends of steel-edge wires and facing wires. When wire ends are slipped into this joiner and the joiners are clamped with wire cutters, there is no chance of the wire ends slipping. A facing edge is much more finished looking when these are used.

3. Threads.

Geneva thread is a strong, smooth, cotton thread with a mercerized finish. It is well adapted to frame wiring and to all millinery sewing except finishes.

Sewing silk for millinery varies little from that used for dressmaking. The best grade is much stronger and better to use because there are fewer breaks and fewer knots to hide.

Embroidery threads are *silk, tinsel, yarn,* and *fiber.* Usually they are heavier than those used for other embroideries.

4. Liquid preparations.

Millinery glue has a great deal of dryer in it because it is chiefly used on velvets and satins which must not mar.

Shellac is a finish used on lisère and other fine, shining straws to restore their lustre after the braid has been sized or soaked.

Gilt and *silver* preparations are used to tint flowers and to metalize wire frames for tinsel hats.

Colorite is used to dye straw hats and braids.

5. Needles.

Embroidery needles with long eyes rounded at the ends are best for millinery purposes. *Crewel* and *chenille* needles are good because the eyes make large holes so that the fabric is not torn by the embroidery thread.

For sewing braids ordinary milliner's needles (a long, strong needle with a large eye) Nos. 4, 5, and 6 are used.

For fine work as for edge finishes and slip-stitching, Nos. 7 and 8 milliner's needles are best.

For frame work Nos. 4 and 5 milliner's needles are best adapted.

For sewing fabric on a frame Nos. 4 and 5 milliner's needles are used.

For trimming no needle is so satisfactory as a No. 4 milliner's needle.

QUESTIONS

1. What are the points of importance in choosing millinery fabrics?
2. How is velvet woven?
3. How does Lyons velvet get its name?
4. What are the most undesirable qualities in straw braids?
5. Define body hats.
6. How and where are leghorns woven?
7. How are panamas woven?
8. What differentiates a beaver felt from other felts?
9. Name the kinds of wire used in millinery.
10. Name the needles used for embroidery, straw sewing, and edge finishes.

CHAPTER VI

CUTTING MATERIALS

I. CUTTING A TRUE BIAS
   How to obtain a true bias
   When a true bias is necessary
   Importance of stretching
   Matching seams
   1. Seam placement
   To cut a correct bias on Lyons velvet
      Rule
II. CUTTING A LONG BIAS
   Process of cutting a long bias
   When a long bias is required
III. TABLE OF BIAS MEASURES
IV. RULES FOR MEASURING MATERIAL FOR A BIAS THAT IS TO BE STRETCHED
   Folds
   Flanges
V. CORRECT SHADING FOR VELVET AND SOLEIL
VI. MEASURING A FRAME FOR THE CORRECT AMOUNT OF MATERIAL
VII. ACCURACY IN CUTTING, A LARGE FACTOR IN COST SAVING
   A paper pattern to be made first
   Correct placing of pattern important in two ways
   1. Correct results
   2. Greatest economy of materials
VIII. METHODS USED FOR CUTTING MALINE
   Maline used for folds
   Maline used for pleatings
   Maline used for rosettes
   Maline used for bows
IX. CUTTING BIAS BINDING FROM FRAME AND CROWN EDGES
   Economy of time

QUESTIONS

I. CUTTING A TRUE BIAS

How to Obtain a True Bias

To cut a true bias lay the length of material flat on the table. Turn the selvage (the warp) of one side back over onto the material even with the cross thread (the woof). When this turned selvage

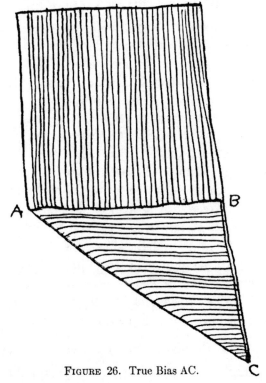

FIGURE 26. True Bias AC.

forms a right angle with the lengthwise selvage, the fold or bias is a true bias and correct for cutting.

In other words, a true bias is the hypotenuse of a right triangle, the other two sides of which are formed by the warp and woof thread of the material.

When a True Bias Is Necessary

An absolutely true bias is necessary when material is to be stretched and fitted on a frame as for a bias flange (see Chapter VII, section II), a bias-stretched fold, a fitted side crown, a milliner's fold.

Importance of Stretching

The fullness at the inner edge (inner circumference) of a bias flange or fold can be worked out only in exact proportion to the amount of stretching done to the outer edge of the flange or fold. The more fullness that is stretched out of the edge the less there will be to work out on the inner circumference.

Matching Seams

Seams on a stretched bias must always run with the warp or selvage. To make a seam on the cross threads or woof is to have a lumpy-looking seam because the seam stitching runs counter to the heavier warp threads. On striped or figured materials the pattern may be made to match just as on a straight seam.

1. Seam placement. In hats all seams should come at the back unless they will be hidden by trimming. When two seams are required (as for velvet folds or flanges on a large-brim edge), place one on each side of the back. Keep them far enough apart so that the extra length does not look like a patch.

To Cut a Correct Bias on Lyons Velvet

In draping hats it is important that bias run the same way. The following rule has been evolved and is uniformly observed by careful workers.

Rule: Place the velvet flat on a table in front of you so that the nap is rough to the left. In turning the bias throw the selvage from you.

CUTTING MATERIALS 67

II. CUTTING A LONG BIAS

Process of Cutting a Long Bias

When cutting a long bias the selvage edge is turned across the material on a long slant forming an obtuse angle with the selvage sides. This gives a much longer bias length (see Figure 27).

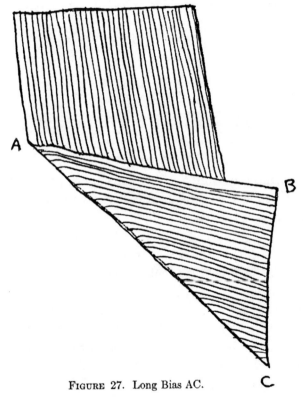

Figure 27. Long Bias AC.

When a Long Bias Is Required

Material, especially Lyons velvet and soleil, is cut on a long bias in order to avoid a piecing when the bias is used to cover a brim plain or in a puff. A long bias is often an advantage in a drape.

III. TABLE OF BIAS MEASURES

The measurement given may be on the selvage or through the strip of bias. Always note which measure is given. The following table is of help in determining the amount of material necessary for a hat.

6 inches on the selvage of a bias	= $4\frac{1}{2}$	inches through the bias.
9 " " " " " " "	= $6\frac{1}{4}$	" " " "
10 " " " " " " "	= $7\frac{1}{4}$	" " " "
12 " " " " " " "	= $8\frac{1}{2}$	" " " "
18 " " " " " " "	= $13\frac{1}{4}$	" " " "
24 " " " " " " "	= 18	" " " "

IV. RULES FOR MEASURING MATERIAL FOR A BIAS WHICH IS TO BE STRETCHED

Folds

In measuring the length of either bias flange or fold, stretch the bias strip (with correct width measure as given below) tightly around the edge of the hat and allow one-half inch on each end for a seam.

Stretch and pin the material to the form as it will be when finished. That is, down the center lengthwise for a fold; on one edge for a flange.

In measuring for a stretched bias fold of not more than one and one-half inches finished, allow three quarters of an inch to be taken up in stretching and one inch for turning under the edges. That is, one and three-quarters inches in all.

For a fold more than one and one-half inches, allow one-half inch more stretch for each inch added in width.

Flanges

In measuring for a stretched bias flange of not more than one and one-quarter inches when finished, allow five eighths of an

CUTTING MATERIALS

inch to be taken up in the stretching and one inch for turning under the edges. That is, one and five-eighths inches in all.

For a flange of more than one and one-quarter inches when finished, allow three quarters of an inch for stretch — one and three-quarters inches in all.

V. CORRECT SHADING FOR VELVET AND SOLEIL

To shade correctly on a fitted hat, velvet or soleil should have the corner or bias of the material at the front and be rough from the face. This is only because the pile is long and has depth of color. When placed in this way the darker and more becoming shade is next the face.

VI. MEASURING A FRAME FOR THE CORRECT AMOUNT OF MATERIAL

This may be done by measuring and computing the amount with a tape measure, or by cutting paper patterns and placing them accurately on a strip of material the width of that to be used, and measuring the strip.

VII. ACCURACY IN CUTTING, A LARGE FACTOR IN COST SAVING

A Paper Pattern to Be Made First

This prevents mistakes in cutting, because all that is experimental about the fitting is worked out on paper. From the paper patterns may be measured the exact amount of material needed. In using expensive fabrics inches saved means dollars saved in cost.

CORRECT PLACING OF PATTERNS IMPORTANT IN TWO WAYS

1. Correct results. The paper patterns should be so placed on the material that a bias comes in the front on a brim, so that the crown material shades the same way as the brim in front when velvet or satin is used.

A bias side crown can shade the same way in only one place

because the entire side crown runs one way. This one place should be the front.

2. Greatest economy of materials. By proper placing of the pattern a great deal of material may be saved. Because of the swing of the brim in fitting, one pattern may be made to fit into the curve of the other. If the material is merely fitted on the brim without making patterns, this advantage is lost.

VIII. METHODS USED FOR CUTTING MALINE

Because maline is merely a series of holes or cells, different methods are used for cutting.

Maline Used for Folds

For **folds** maline is cut on the straight lengthwise. This avoids the use of more than one seam. A bias is not needed, for the open mesh allows for all the give necessary. A bias would warp out of shape and stretch to a string.

Maline Used for Pleatings

For **pleatings** where much cutting is to be done have the material folded once, as it comes, and pin it up to a 10- or 12-inch length. Pin flat on the center fold and smooth out all fullness or wrinkles. Then cut the strips for pleatings. Take out the pins and separate the strips.

For a trimming of pleatings the maline should be folded over.

For a brim-pleated ruffle maline is usually cut into three strips and each strip folded double before pleating. The original center fold of maline makes the fold of one strip.

For a side-crown trimming of many rows or pleated rosettes maline is ordinarily cut into six strips. Each strip is folded over before pleating into a dovetail rosette. This is then sewed to the side crown on a rosette foundation.

Maline Used for Rosettes

For **large rosettes** the full width of maline is often sewed in close loops to a twisted length of cable wire or a tab. The loops must be very close and sewed on both sides of the foundation.

The loops are then spread out the full width and clipped all around with sharp scissors. This gives a ball-like rosette.

Maline Used for Bows

For **bows** of maline the full width should be folded and made over a foundation form of cable wire. The wire may be looped in a regular bow effect (like a lover's-knot bow) and the maline tacked over it.

Always use soft, loose knots in maline bows.

Always handle maline as little as possible. Handling crushes it.

Always use a moderately hot iron. Too hot an iron melts the sizing and tears the mesh of the maline.

IX. CUTTING BIAS BINDING FOR FRAME AND CROWN EDGES

Economy of Time

Economy of time in cutting is an important item in a large workroom. When the correct method is used, one girl can cut enough crinoline or mull to last for weeks, in a few minutes. Cut a bias corner from the length of binding material. Fold back five inches of material lengthwise (on the bias edge). Turn this again and again until the full width is folded. This will give all the bias edge folded together in one space of five inches. Fold and flatten the entire length of material, which may be five or six yards long. Place pins at intervals of a few inches. The selvage will wind in a bias slant around the fold. With a sharp pair of scissors cut one-inch strips from the top, folded, bias edge.

The best materials for frame and crown edges are crinoline, cotton, mull, or lightweight muslin. When the entire amount of binding is cut, wind it into flat rolls ready for use. Before binding an edge always stretch each bias strip so that there is no slack in it. This gives a smoother surface.

QUESTIONS

1. Give directions for cutting a true bias.
2. Give directions for cutting a long bias.
3. When is each necessary?
4. Give the rules for measuring material for a stretched bias fold.
5. How may material for a hat be cut most economically?
6. How does maline cutting differ from that of other materials? Why?
7. What is the correct way to shade velvet?
8. How is bias frame binding cut?

CHAPTER VII

THE FABRIC HAT

I. Fall Materials and Fabrics
Velvet
Satin soleil
Plushes
   1. Hatter's plush
   2. French plush
Satin
   1. Baronet satin
   2. Brocaded satin
   3. Duchess satin
Duvetyn
Fancy materials
   1. Brocades
   2. Tapestries
   3. Chinese embroideries and embroidery medallions
Furs
   1. Seal
   2. Martin
   3. Beaver
   4. Mole
   5. Monkey
   6. Astrakhan
   7. Kolinsky
Ribbons
Braids
   1. Chenille
   2. Felt
   3. Yarn

II. Classified Construction of Fabric Hats for Fall and Winter
Drapes
    1. Matron's turbans
    2. Harem turbans
Semidrapes
    1. Section hats
    2. Tams
    3. Saddle tams
Fitted hats
    1. Fitted, unpasted hats
    2. Fitted, pasted hats
Sewing fur
    1. Fitting
    2. Cutting
    3. Sewing
    4. Equipment needed
Questions

I. FALL MATERIALS AND FABRICS

Velvet*

Velvet has more gorgeous color effects than any other fabric because of its deep silk pile which gives depth of light and shadow. The shadows cause one color to have many different tints.

Satin Soleil

Satin soleil in black is one of the smartest materials for tailored hats.

As it comes, too, in all the velvet shades, velvet and soleil in matching shades make a handsome hat because of the contrast of the high lustre of soleil and the soft, dull finish of velvet.

Plushes

1. Hatter's plush. Hatter's plush is similar in finish to soleil but has a much longer nap. It is used for strictly tailored hats and is usually shown in street shades.

*See Chapter V, section I, page 51.

THE FABRIC HAT

2. French plush. French plush is similar in finish to a fine coat plush. Though the pile is thick and deep and soft, the material is very lightweight. It is used in combination with satin, satin soleil, or velvet for tailored hats in street shades.

SATIN

Satin is a favored fabric for late fall and early spring hats.

1. Baronet satin. Baronet is a fiber satin with a high, almost metallic finish which combines beautifully with plush and with polished straws. Because of its lustre it makes a good background for beadwork and embroidery. Many smart hats for midseason wear are made of baronet satin.

2. Brocaded satin. Brocaded satin in black, white, and colors with silver and gold thread woven in is used for small winter hats. Harem and semidraped turbans of this fabric are very good to wear with furs and fur coats.

3. Duchess satin. Duchess satin in street shades is used for draped and tailored hats and in combination with velvet, soleil, and straw for fall and early winter hats.

DUVETYN

Duvetyn is one of the most satisfactory fabrics for fall sport and tailored hats. Its soft texture makes it effective for drapes in tailored hats. The dull finish and beautiful shades make good background for yarn and chenille embroidery.

FANCY MATERIALS

1. Brocades. Brocades in gold, silver, tinsel, satin mixtures, velvet, chiffons, and georgettes are very handsome. These are used largely for formal afternoon and evening hats.

Draped and semidraped hats combine brocades with plain velvets, satins, and furs. Ordinarily these hats are small or medium in size.

2. Tapestries. Imported Chinese, Swiss, and French tapestries are beautiful in coloring and very lightweight. These, too, are combined with plain velvets and satins in harmonizing colors. They are used in designs for semidress, dressy afternoon, and evening hats.

3. Chinese embroideries from Mandarin robes and **embroidery medallions** are used on satin pokes and Napoleons, on velvet-brim hats, on maline and velvet combinations, and occasionally to form entire turbans. The colors and work make very rich and effective models.

FURS

Fur is seldom used for entire hats because of the weight and heat. Fur crowns are apt to be too heavy-looking for present-day fashions.

Fur facings, fur edges, and fur trimmings are very smart.

1. Seal. Seal is often used for entire brims in small hats, for irregular-fitted flanges, for rolled edges, and for cut-out work with beads and tinsel threads.

2. Martin. Martin is used for coronets on small turbans, for edges on small, up-turned brims, and occasionally for edges.

Baby martin is better fitted for millinery than any other fur because it is lighter weight and softer.

3. Beaver. Beaver is used in the same way as seal (see above).

4. Mole. Mole, because it is lightweight and short-furred, makes entire crowns and small hats. It combines beautifully with brocades and satins. Wooden beads, brocade, tinsel thread, and mole are sometimes combined in an embroidery on satin hats.

5. Monkey. Monkey is used in banding for edges on velvet, satin, and maline hats. It may be arranged in fanciful designs for ornaments to give aigrette-like effects.

6. Astrakhan. Astrakhan is used for facings on turned-up brims, for a few entire turbans, and in combination with satin on small hats.

7. Kolinsky. Kolinsky is used in the same way as martin (see page 76).

Ribbons

Both wide and narrow ribbons are used for entire hats in sport and tailored models.

Children's hats and rain hats may be made from moiré ribbon, which is very durable.

Braids *

1. Chenille. Chenille braid is used for entire hats in sports and tailored designs. Some of the fancy patterns of braid are combined with ribbonzene, narrow chenille, or yarn for embroidery work.

2. Felt. Felt braids come in narrow and wide patterns for sport hats.

3. Yarn. Yarn braids are used for entire sport hats, for edges on felt hats, and for embroidery work on sport hats.

II. CLASSIFIED CONSTRUCTION OF FABRIC HATS FOR FALL AND WINTER

Drapes

Draped hats are like French frocks, apparently simple but in reality the last word in clever design and workmanship.

No one, no matter how talented, need expect to make finished and professional-looking draped hats without a great deal of practice.

Not everyone can succeed in being a trimmer or designer.

*See Lesson VIII, section II, page 93.

But anyone who is willing to work faithfully and to practice long enough can acquire deftness and skill that will enable her to copy designs, to do exquisite making, to drape a hat in soft, loose folds, to sew on trimming in a faultless manner. In other words, anyone who has average intelligence and who wills it may train her eyes to see and her hands to do what the mind directs.

FIGURE 28. Draped Turban with Bias Side Crown.

Draped hats, more than any other type, need deftness of touch. The folds must be well secured but must look smooth and soft without any stitches showing anywhere.

For the average worker it is best to pin the entire drape first and tack it later. She may then adjust and readjust until the desired effect is obtained.

1. Matron's turbans. Much is said elsewhere of matron's turbans (see Chapter X, section I).

There are three invariably necessary qualities for a successful and becoming turban for the older girl and woman: (1) correct headsize; (2) a soft roll or tiny headsize brim; (3) softness.

A good method of practice is to prepare a soft, oval crown by adding a headsize binding of elastic net or an inch brim, and cutting a $\frac{7}{8}$-yard length of velvet, one end bias and one end straight. Drape this in as many and as varied ways as possible. The simplest manner is to wind the bias around the headsize (slanting the true bias into a long bias if the brim needs more length to cover it) and pull the length around the crown into folds or pleats. The straight end may be finished in a series of shirrings to form a rosette or it may be laid in pleats and finished with a ribbon ornament, or with flowers or feathers, or a bow. The possibilities are endless.

Another safe drape is made by covering the headsize brim or coronet with a drape of bias folds, or covering it with an undraped bias which has been beaded or embroidered.

Then drape the top crown with an oval of velvet laid in loose folds or shirred a little at the center.

FIGURE 29. Draped Turban with Bias Side Crown.

Cover the side crown with shirred rosettes of ribbon, or velvet, or with a feather band.

A plain nine-inch bias of velvet may be draped in folds around the crown, as for a side crown, and wings or flowers to match the velvet, posed in groups around the crown.

2. **Harem turbans.** (See Chapter X, section II.)

FIGURE 30. Harem Turban with Section Top Crown.

SEMIDRAPES

Under this division come the simplest and some of the loveliest hats made; simple because exact patterns for crown and brim in one can be given; and lovely because they are soft and smart and make good background for much pleasing handwork.

1. Sectional hats. Sectional hats are usually sewn from the crown center down to the headsize. Seams may be plain, corded, or finished with fancy stitching. They may be made of velvet, satin soleil, or any fabric with body. Only very soft fabrics need an interlining.

Four-sectional. Four-sectional hats may be shaped tams draped over a crown, or they may have a brim extension which turns up all around the crown. The latter are sometimes draped over rolled brims. Sometimes the fabric simply rolls up around the crown without a brim frame.

Exact dimensions and directions are always given with the patterns.

Six-sectional. Six-sectional draped hats make good semitailored and sport hats. They may be of silk fabric, velvet, satin soleil, wide ribbon, or silk sports cloth. Narrow ribbon may be sewn horizontally in strips the width of the section pattern. Sections are cut from this, and the hat assembled in the usual way. This design gives a gay air of the unusual which is charming.

FIGURE 31. Two-Sectional Draped Hat.

Two-sectional. Two-sectional hats may be tams or may have the effect of brim and crown. Directions are always given with the pattern.

This type of hat makes a remarkably good design for young girls and is easy for beginning milliners to make. The results are satisfactory in either case.

THE FABRIC HAT

2. Tams. (See Chapter X, section III.) Draped tams are almost universally becoming. The soft width may always be becomingly adjusted to the individual face.

Here again, practice in draping makes for perfection of results. The tam drape must not look tight or pasted, nor can it be too loose and careless.

It is always well to adjust the drape carefully and to tack with the fewest possible stitches. A tie tack is commonly used for this. The ends of the thread are tied from inside the crown and the stitch caught through the under side of a fold on the outside.

Circular or fitted. A circular tam may have a round or oval top. The outside is usually semi-circular with the outer segment of the circle attached to the outer edge of the circle top. *Seams.* Since most tams drape lower at the right side than anywhere else, the seam is usually at the right side.

FIGURE 32. Six-Sectional Draped Hat.

Directions are always given with each pattern.

Sectional tams.

a. Four-sectional tams. Four-sectional tams are cut in two distinct manners: (1) to give a decided sectional effect; (2) to show no seams but to give desired effect for the shape of the drape. It will readily be seen that four seams give much help in attaining a desired shape.

b. Six-sectional tams. Six-sectional tams are usually for misses and juniors. Soft and unusual effects are easily obtained.

Embroidery, ribbon ornaments, or quills may serve as trimming (see Chapter X, section III).

FIGURE 33. Four-Sectional Tam.   FIGURE 34. Four-Sectional Draped Hat.

3. Saddle tams. Saddle tams have a shaped section running from side to side across the top of the hat. The front and back may be in one or two sections each. The shaping gives an unusual line for drape.

The construction is easy and therefore furnishes a good problem for the beginner.

FITTED HATS

Fitted hats are divided into two general classes — pasted and unpasted. Because of the present popularity of soft hats there are few pasted hats. Paste is used to hold material to a concave surface, but otherwise it is not frequently used.

1. Fitted, unpasted hats. This classification includes most of the brim hats. The fabric is fitted over a brim and sewn at the headsize and edge. Mushrooms, turned-up brims, pokes, and

THE FABRIC HAT

small sailors are usually fitted and covered in the same way. Turned-up brims may have the top or the facing put on first, but the processes are the same.

Edge finishes:

a. Plain, wire edges. These are the edges commonly used in fitted hats. The under facing is fitted to the frame and sewn to the headsize with a backstitch.

The seam, if any, may be slip-stitched before or after the edge wire is pinned in. Starting at the right-side back, pin the edge of the material over and under a facing wire, placing the pins just under the wire in the material and through the frame. Pin only half the facing in this manner.

FIGURE 35. Saddle Tam.

Sew by running the needle along under the wire to form a groove for the placement of stitches, which should be not more than one-fourth inch underneath. Slant the needle through the material to the edge and back without any stitches on top. The

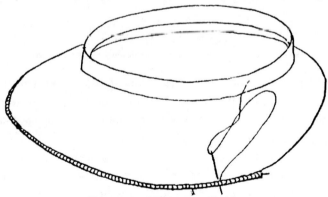

FIGURE 36. Edge-Wire Finish.
Note that there is no stitch on the top — only between the hat edge and the cord.

thread from under the wire to the edge above should be brought back (by the needle) under the wire. Thus it forms a stitch which does not show when the thread is pulled tight.

When half the facing is finished, pin the other half and sew, leaving a two-inch space open for the wire joining. When ready for this, cut the two ends of the wire evenly and slip a wire joiner

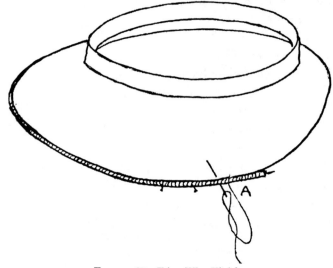

FIGURE 37. Edge-Wire Finish.
The position of the needle shows the way in which the stitches travel.

on to hold the two ends. A wire joiner is made like the tip of a shoe lace (not a bad substitute) and may be bought in any good department store. Sew over the wire joiner and sew the material to the frame headsize with a whip-stitch.

b. Slip-stitched edges. The top facing is fitted and pinned in place. The center slashes are sewn at the headsize with a backstitch, which is run just above the headsize bend or wire. The edge is carefully fitted, and pins are adjusted to hold it in place.

A quarter-inch or half-inch seam is trimmed and caught down on the under side of the frame with a whip-stitch. Stitches must be close together so as to hold the edge flat. No stitches should show on the top. The needle is stuck through the fabric and frame — not through to the fabric on top.

The seam is turned under on each side and slip-stitched from headsize to edge by taking a hidden stitch in first one side and then the other. The needle must always enter one fold in a line exactly opposite the point from which it was pulled from the other side. Pull the thread so that it holds the seam together but not tight enough to pucker it.

FIGURE 38. Brim Hat with Flange Edge.

c. Flange edges. When flange edges are used, the facing (top or under, whichever is used) is sewn at the headsize as usual, and at the outer edge, which extends out on the frame so that it laps one-half inch under the flange. It is pinned flat, and sewn with a backstitch. The stitches may be half an inch long, but must be tight so that no fullness accumulates under them.

The flange may be bias or fitted. Directions are always given on the pattern. In either case the edge is sewn as for a plain, fitted hat (see above).

The inner edge of the flange is pinned over a wire as for a facing edge (see *Edge finishes* above).

The only difference in sewing is that the needle may be stuck through the frame as the stitches showing there are hidden by the facing. Take a small stitch close under the wire and a small one on the under brim. Use a matching silk thread. When there are but five or six inches left to sew, clip the wire ends, slip on the joiner, and clamp it over the wire ends well.

Do not put the joiner under a seam. It will show less where there is no extra thickness. Finish sewing the flange.

Put in the facing as for a plain, fitted edge.

d. Fold edges. Fitted, fold edges finish the hat so that the raw edge of facings, both top and bottom, are sewn flat at the brim edge (or near the edge) of the hat with a backstitch as for a flange (see *Flange edges* above).

When tailored stiff hats are in vogue, there are many bias-edge folds used as finishes. These are put on as a flange is put on, except that there is no edge-wire finish. The bias strip of material is folded over the raw edges of the facing. The inner edge of bias material is finished over a wire or cord as a flange is finished.

Care must be used to keep the top and bottom wires even, so that the stitches of one may be slanted under the wire of the other.

(1) Loose folds. Since soft edges are becoming, loose folds are very popular. After the top brim is put on and before the facing is put in, a bias fold of material is fitted around the edge of the hat (with the fold edge extending out). The two raw edges of the fold are sewn down to the frame over the raw edge of the top facing. It is best to pin, fit, and seam the fold before sewing it. Seams should be placed at either side of the back when more than one is necessary. Otherwise, the seam is directly at the back. The facing edge is finished just as for a plain, fitted hat. Many maline fold edges are put on dress hats in this manner.

(2) Extended folds. The raw edges of the bias fold may be held slightly full so that the outer edge extends beyond the frame edge. These folds are usually $\frac{3}{4}$ to $1\frac{1}{2}$ inches finished.

THE FABRIC HAT 87

(3) Turned-back folds. These folds are usually $\frac{1}{2}$ to $\frac{3}{4}$ inch finished. The fold may be turned back over the top brim merely to give a soft-edge effect. In this case turn the folded edge back over the top and stretch the raw edges as the fold is pinned in place at the facing edge. This makes the fold edge lie flat without any fullness.

e. Machine-stitched and turned edges. This is one of the simplest edge finishes and is used by the better factories. Both

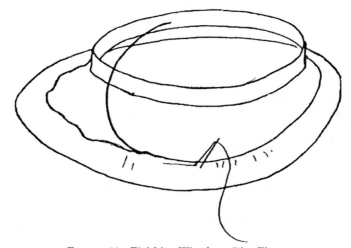

FIGURE 39. Finishing Wire for a Bias Flange.

top and under facings are sewn at the headsize and trimmed and sewn flat and even with the frame edge.

A bias fold is measured around the frame edge, allowing no fullness; and for a small hat, stretching the bias just a little. The seams are joined after the fold is fitted. The two raw edges must be brought together and basted so that the fold lies flat and even. The fold, when finished, may be from $\frac{3}{4}$ to $1\frac{1}{4}$ inches wide. Pin the two raw edges even with the frame edge on the under side of the brim. Sew with a tight backstitch. Then turn the fold over onto the top of the brim. Factories sew this with a straw-sewing machine rather than by hand.

2. Fitted, pasted hats.

Machine-pasted hats. Most machine-made velvet and many silk hats are pasted. These include many of the larger cheap velvet hats.

Knox sailors and many of the smart tailored-velvet and satin-soleil hats are pasted and pressed by machine. These have ribbon-edge bindings or glued-wire finishes.

Hand-pasted hats. In making a pasted hat, the facings are fitted and sewn at the headsize. The glue is then smeared evenly over the frame, a section (about a quarter of the brim) at a time. The material is carefully smoothed over the glue by rubbing with the hand from the headsize out to the edge. If fullness is accidentally left in, pull the material loose before the glue dries and smooth it over again.

FIGURE 40. Finished Hat with a Turned-over Fold Edge.

Be careful to purchase a good quality of millinery glue or cement. Ordinary glue mars the fabric.

Do not try to paste any fabric which has not much body. Velvet, satin soleil, suede cloth, duvetyn, heavy satin, moiré, and heavy faille are about the only fabrics that will not mar when paste is used.

THE FABRIC HAT

Sewing Fur

In sewing fur remember (1) that the fur should always run the same way; (2) that a richer light is given when the fur shades rough; (3) that the hair must not be cut off in cutting the skin.

1. Fitting. In fitting a fur hat use a pattern for the space, or crown, or facing to be fitted. Pin the fur to the pattern wrong side

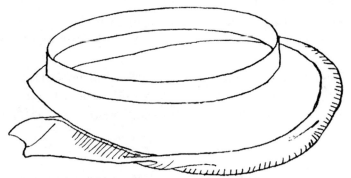

FIGURE 41. A Turned-over Fold-edge Finish.

out to join the seams. Before the last seam is joined, pin the fur to the frame, stretching it smooth, and take out any extra fullness in the last seam.

To get the best results, the hide side of the fur pelt should be dampened (not the fur) and the skin stretched and tacked fur side down on a table or board to dry. This gives a larger surface, saving fur and detracting from the weight per square inch. Banding already made does not need stretching.

2. Cutting. Fur should always be marked with pencil or chalk on the skin side and cut with a knife on the marking line. A safety-razor blade is a good substitute for a fur knife. Hold the fur so that the fur hair will not be cut when the skin is.

3. Sewing. Hold the two edges of skin to be sewed together with all the hair pushed inside. Sew with whip stitches or overcasting stitches so close together that the seam stands up in a cord.

If the hair has not been cut and the two pieces of fur shade the same way, the fur can be sewn so that the seam does not show on the right side.

After the seams are finished, whip a narrow tape to the outer edge of the fur with close, fine stitches. Use this tape to sew to the hat frame or to turn back and whip down onto the skin back for a band or bow of fur. Bows of fur may have silk facings slip-stitched to this tape.

4. Equipment needed. Thumb tacks; razor blades; chalk; strong, fine, cotton thread (Geneva No. 40 is good); and short, strong needles are all the equipment that is necessary for fur work in millinery.

QUESTIONS

1. What are the important points in making matrons' draped hats?
2. Make two doll-size draped hats.
3. Why are draped tams so universally becoming?
4. What frames are used for two-, four-, and six-sectional hats?
5. Make a sectional hat from cotton flannel or silkoline, constructing the original pattern and a simple embroidery design.
6. Make a set of five circles, four inches in diameter, with a different finish for each edge. Use frame material for these circle foundations; wire, and finish as for a hat.
7. Why should fur pelts be stretched before cutting?
8. How is fur cut?

CHAPTER VIII

BRAID HATS

I. KINDS
   Summer braids
      1. Visca braid
      2. Satin straw
      3. Hemp braid
      4. Milan braid
      5. Lisère braid
      6. Tuscan braid
   Sport braids
      1. Yarn braid
      2. Chenille braid
      3. Felt braid
      4. Ramie braid
   Hair braid
      1. Plain hair
      2. Hair braids with designs
      3. Hair braid folded by machine
      4. Hair tubing
      5. Fancy weaves of hair braids

II. MANNER OF SEWING
   Crowns
      1. Molding a soft crown over a wooden or buckram block
      2. Sewing braid to a pressed crown
   Plain brim
      1. With a frame
      2. Without a frame
   Fancy sewing of braid brims in designs
   Fancy crown sewing

Sewing milan and lisère
1. Soaking braid
2. Molding over wire frame
3. Molding over wooden blocks
4. Drying braid
5. Shellac finish

QUESTIONS

The manufacture of braids for millinery forms an extensive industry on the Continent. In the United States most of the industry is confined to the eastern manufacturing group of states where immigrant labor is used.

I. KINDS

There are, of course, more kinds of braids for summer wear than for fall and winter. Braid hats for fall are almost invariably for sport wear.

SUMMER BRAIDS

1. Visca braid. Visca braid is soft and pliable, well-suited to classroom work because it is easily handled.

2. Satin straw. Satin straw is woven of a composition with such a smooth and shining surface that it has the appearance of hard candy.

3. Hemp braid. Hemp makes lovely sport hats when combined with ribbon. It is very satisfactory for facings in fabric hats for early spring and late summer as it is smooth and finished-looking.

4. Milan braid. Milan braid makes some of the smartest of the spring hats. It is an expensive braid both from the point of cost of material and of labor, but is well worth the cost. The sewing gives interesting construction problems for the classroom.

5. Lisère braid. Lisère braid has a harder finish and more of a shine than milan braid. For feather-trimmed, tailored hats and for celophane and lacquered, plume-trimmed hats it is very handsome. Lisère stripping is used for combination sewing with hair braid.

6. Tuscan braid. Tuscan braid is used for elaborate sport and lingerie hats. Special patterns are made for embroidery use. In these patterns the design is practically complete and ready to be applied to hats of straw cloth or fabric.

Sport Braids

1. Yarn braid. Yarn braid comes in plain and mixed colors suitable for sport wear. Entire hats are often made of and trimmed with yarn braid.

Flowers may be made of assorted colors and used on plain-colored hats. For example: rust, jade, copenhagen blue, henna, and dull, purple flowers may be used on a sand-colored yarn-braid hat with darker tan-yarn stitching.

2. Chenille braid. Chenille braid comes in more elaborate designs than yarn braid. Often a floral pattern in colors is woven in the braid. This makes it adaptable for trimming purposes. Other patterns are woven of wired chenille. These braids may be sewn without a frame. The body of the braid is sufficient to hold them in shape.

3. Felt braid. Felt braid is much used for machine-sewed sport hats. The edge of the braid is often cut in a pattern of points and scallops.

4. Ramie braid is manufactured from the Malay grass-cloth plant. The strong, rough texture makes it a favorite among manufacturers.

Hair Braid

Hair braid is much favored for early spring and summer wear. The spring hats are sewed on pressed frames over a silk or silkoline covering (or interlining). Satin or taffeta is used for crowns or facings.

1. Plain hair. There are three distinct qualities of plain hair braid.

Swiss hair braid is the best quality. It has a lovely lustre, a good fiber, and is closely woven.

German hair braid has a poorer fiber than Swiss hair. The lustre is metallic and the weave, loose and less perfect.

Domestic hair braid is the poorest quality. It is limp, coarse, and lustreless. Most of the cheap factory-made hair hats are made of this.

2. Hair braids with designs come in patterns of exquisite texture and workmanship. These braids are made in Switzerland and France and are used for garden hats and for dressy, all-black hats combined with maline.

White hair with designs in natural tuscan has a dainty effect very pretty in combination with chiffon, georgette, or lace for lingerie or flower-trimmed hats.

Designs in visca on hair braid are used on black, brown, sand, and navy hair-braid hats suitable for both dress and tailored designs.

Designs of satin straw on hair braid come in both street and pastel shades. These braids are suitable for plainer dress and street models.

Designs of embroidery in raffia straw and silk threads on plain hair come in elaborate designs for dressy, tailored, and plainer dress hats.

3. Hair braid folded by machine makes soft effects for facing and is used for street and semidress hats. Plain hair braid or silk are used in combination to prevent the hat from being thick-looking.

4. **Hair tubing** comes in many colors and is used for braiding and embroidering on plain hair, on silk fabrics, and on straw cloths.

5. **Fancy weaves of hair braid** (that is, hair braid woven in scallops and irregular patterns) come in a variety of designs suitable for both dress and tailored models.

II. MANNER OF SEWING

The manner of sewing braid varies, but the simplest and most effective methods are the ones given.

CROWNS

Crowns may be sewn in the hand while shaping them into tam or round crowns. In this method the eye must be well trained. The most satisfactory methods for students are:

1. Molding a soft crown over a wooden or buckram block. Wooden molds are an advantage because they may be used for steaming crowns into shape. Buckram crowns will serve as molds for braid sewing but soften with the use of steam.

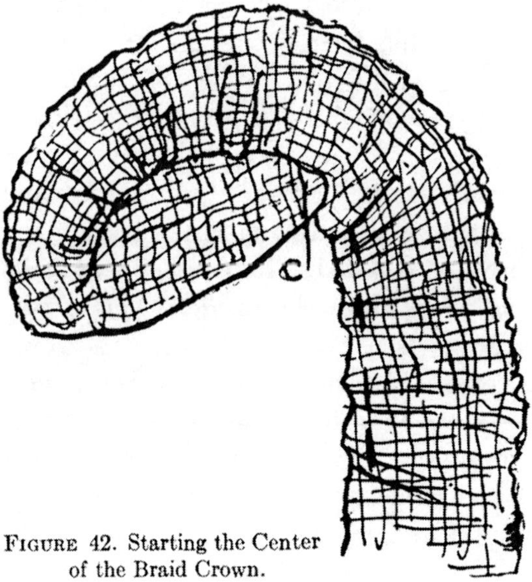

FIGURE 42. Starting the Center of the Braid Crown.

In sewing a braid crown start sewing at the center top of the crown. Pull up the draw thread at one end of the braid. (If the braid has no draw string, run one in with a shirring.) Curve the braid in a lengthened circle or oval. Turn back one end for a finish. The center should be a finished oval with braid edge forming the oval edge.

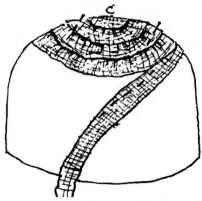

FIGURE 43. Molding a Braid Crown.

Lap the selvage of the braid under the edge of the preceding row. Pull up the draw string just enough to make the edge curve to fit the crown or mold. Slide the needle under the braid. Take a small hidden stitch on top and a longer stitch on the wrong side. Do not stitch through the frame at any time. When the top oval has been sewn almost as large as the top of the crown, press it with a moderately hot iron on the wrong side. Then pin it in place on the top of the buckram crown. If a wooden mold is used, fasten it with thumb tacks. Continue sewing down row after row until the base of the crown is reached. Remove pins or tacks and press from the inside. This crown may be used over a soft, pressed crown or over a headsize band as foundation.

2. Sewing braid to a pressed crown. Sewing braid to a pressed crown is done in the same way, except that the stitches are taken through the crown after the tip

FIGURE 44. Braid Hat with Fabric Facing. Molded Braid Crown with Side-Crown Foundation.

is started in the hand. Very tight stitches may be taken because the crown holds them in place. Use long stitches inside the crown and small hidden stitches on the outside.

BRAID HATS

Plain Brim

1. **With a frame.** Bind the frame edge with a row of braid or 1-inch bias strip of silk.

Sew the first row of braid flat over the binding. Allow only ⅛ inch of silk to show. Start the first row a little to one side of the back so that there is room to lap the second row over the end of the first at a gradual slant. Pull up the thread on the inner edge. Continue sewing row after row until the headsize is reached.

Irregular brims will need extra rows at the wider parts.

Always sew the outer rows first and fill in the extra rows at the headsize.

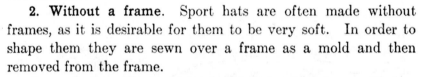

Figure 45. Starting the First Row of Braid as a Binding on the Edge of the Brim.

2. **Without a frame.** Sport hats are often made without frames, as it is desirable for them to be very soft. In order to shape them they are sewn over a frame as a mold and then removed from the frame.

For such hats the braid is sewn by slanting the needle (not sticking through the frame). Then the braid can be removed from the frame and the edge wired. Sew the under facing in the same way. Remove from the frame and join the top and under brims at the edge.

Sew the crown over a mold (see section II, above) and attach it to the brim at the headsize.

If the brim is an even shape, the crown may be sewn to the

brim and the braid sewn from top crown to brim edge in one piece.

Fancy Sewing of Braid Brims in Designs

In sewing dress hats of hair, lisère, milan, and visca braid the braid is often sewn in designs of scallops, loops, and points. Individual patterns give the designs used.

Fancy Crown Sewing

The narrower braids are often sewn in designs as part of the trimming for semitailored models. The braid designs are given with the patterns.

Sewing Milan and Lisère

Milan and lisère have a harder finish than any other braids. They have enough body so that the braid when sewn will hold together without a frame but must be soaked in water in order that one may sew them without breaking the straw.

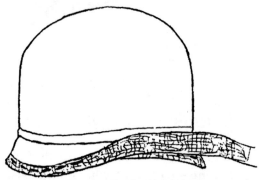
Figure 46. Slanting the Braid for the Second Row.

1. Soaking braid. This means merely soaking the braid in warm water before sewing it. Allow the braid to be submerged for about five minutes. Shake off the loose water and wrap the braid in newspaper or a towel. It is then ready for sewing.

2. Molding over wire frame. The soaked lisère or milan may be molded over a wire frame (brim or crown). Bind the edge of the frame with any cotton material. Baste the first row of braid to the binding with long stitches that are easily pulled out when the hat is dry.

Sew the braid over the wire frame just as on a pressed frame. Slant the second row over the end of the first at the back. Sew the second row to the first and the third to the second. Continue to the headsize. Be careful not to stitch over the wires or the threads will break when the braid is removed from the frame. Do not stretch the braid tightly on the wire frame or it will draw the frame out of shape and the braid will have a poor line.

3. Molding over wooden blocks. For a crown, shape and sew the soaked braid over a wooden block just as for a soft crown. Split or rip the braid in half for the center tip. When the center oval has a small diameter of 1 inch, use the entire width of braid (see section II, above). When the braid has been shaped over the crown, fasten it at the headsize with thumb tacks and let it remain on the block until dry.

Brims may be sewn over wooden blocks by fastening the first row of braid with thumb tacks and sewing each row of braid to the one preceding it.

A buckram brim will serve the purpose of a wooden mold and hold in shape for sewing three or four hats.

4. Drying braid. Always be sure that the braid is thoroughly dry before removing it from the mold or frame. It loses its shape if it is still damp. The dampness will spoil the shellac finish.

5. Shellac finish. Shellac for braids is a specially prepared shellac for millinery purposes. It dries quickly and is lightweight. Black and transparent shellac are used more than colors. The transparent kind may be used for all colors.

A coat of shellac restores the shine which is lost in soaking braids.

QUESTIONS

1. Name braids suitable for dress hats for early spring; for dressy midsummer wear; for sport wear.
2. What is the best grade of hair braid?
3. What braids are used in combination with hair braid?
4. What is celophane braid?
5. Why are lisère and milan braids soaked before sewing?
6. How are braid crowns sewed? Give steps and illustrations.
7. Can braid hats be made without frames?
8. What is ramie braid? What is tuscan braid? What is lisère braid? What is hair braid?
9. Give all the steps used in sewing milan or lisère braid over a wire frame.
10. What straw braids are used for braiding and embroidery designs?

CHAPTER IX

TRANSPARENT HATS

I. KINDS
   Maline
   1. With brims fitted over wire frames
   2. With steamed crowns
   3. Solid crowns with transparent maline brims
   Lace
   1. Metal lace
   2. Valenciennes lace
   3. Lace flouncing
   4. All-over lace
   Lace and fabric combinations
   Georgette

II. PREPARING THE FRAME
   Winding with maline for black and white hats
   Dyeing to match metal or colored lace
   Metallizing for metal-lace hats

III. EDGE FINISHES
   Braid edges
   Ribbon edges
   Flanges
   1. Velvet
   2. Taffeta
   3. Maline

IV. APPROPRIATE TRIMMINGS
   Lace bows
   Velvet
   Flowers
   1. Silk
   2. Linen
   3. Metal

    4. Velvet
    5. Handmade
   Rosettes
    1. Maline
    2. Ribbon
    3. Taffeta
    4. Velvet
   Feathers
    Questions

Very few wire crowns are used in any hats today because of their discomfort and stiffness. Fabric crowns or soft pressed crowns are more comfortable and much prettier.

There are, among the new styles, many semitransparent hats — that is, hats with lace- or maline-extended soft edges (see illustration, Figure 50). The processes involved in making these are not different from the processes of making the ordinary fabric and straw hats. It means only that a fold of maline or a ruffle of lace is added before the facing is put in. The directions given for maline hats apply as well to net or all-over-lace hats.

I. KINDS

Hair-braid transparent hats are not discussed here, since the preparation is the same as for lace hats and the method of sewing the same as for any braid hats.

Maline

A waterproof maline of closely woven quality is always the best choice, as it wears better, looks much better, and is easier to work with. A coarse maline costs less per yard, but so many more thicknesses of the coarse quality are required than of the fine that the difference in yardage makes the cost practically the same.

Maline is so porous a net, being merely a very fine net with a large amount of sizing or starch, that it is never necessary to cut it on the bias.

1. **With brims fitted over wire frames.** (See section II of this chapter for frame preparation.)

All maline. Maline is fitted over a wire frame in much the same manner as any fabric is fitted over a pressed frame, with a few exceptions.

Fullness in the fitting of an extreme shape with decided curves may be steamed out by holding the hat over steam and stretching out the fullness while the material is damp.

Care must be used in slashing the material at the headsize. If it is cut too deeply, the slash spreads. The better method is always to cut down about half as far as seems necessary. It is always an easy matter to cut farther and difficult to repair a slash cut too deeply. If you have made the mistake of slashing too deep, slip a small piece, 1½ inches wide by 2 inches long, in between the layers of maline at the slash. Do not sew this slipped-in section any place except at the base of the headsize. The facings of maline will hold it in place.

A fine silk wire (French wire) or heavy satin cable wire makes a nicer facing edge or flange finish than brace wire. Cotton wire should never be used for maline hats in any way.

Maline and straw. Maline crowns and extended flange edges may be used with straw brims.

Entire maline hats may be combined with fine straw, as milan, hemp, or visca stripping, sewn over the material in rows ½ inch or more apart.

Other maline fitted hats are covered entirely with a conventional floral design or an angle design of any fine straw tubing or stripping. In these hats the top brim facing of maline is fitted over the wire frame, the crown made and sewn on, and the entire braid design embroidered before the under facing is put in. It serves as a finish to hide the braiding stitches. Matching silk thread is always used. In most cases the stitches may be partially hidden in the braid.

Strips of wide braid, about ½ inch, are sometimes sewn over fitted maline brims from edge to headsize in a stripe effect. The edge may then be finished with a braid or maline fold or a braid fold plus an extended maline edge.

Maline and velvet. Satin or taffeta are often used in the same relative manner as velvet. Many of the better winter dress hats are always made of maline and velvet. The combination makes a perfect background for paradise, ostrich, goura, aigrettes, and handmade flowers. The lustre of velvet and the duller finish of maline make a rich contrast.

FIGURE 47.

Maline brims may have velvet crowns and velvet fitted flanges or bias extended folds. Fitted flanges put on in a design of scallops, squares, or points make handsome finishes and are the last word in needlework accomplishment.

Maline and lace. Maline and lace in combination make a satisfactory dress hat for summer and one which may be used for evening wear all the year round.

All black lace hats need maline for brim facings and crown linings.

Black lace and maline hats are charming when trimmed with large velvet bows or with bands and bows of wide, colored velvet ribbon, as copenhagen blue or begonia shades. Wreaths of field flowers, primroses, corn flowers, heather, or mixed flowers make a black lace and maline hat into a most satisfactory garden hat.

2. With steamed crowns. With steamed crowns a shaped maline crown is made by stretching and steaming maline over a wooden crown mold. This eliminates pleats and shirrings and gives the crown shape without fullness. In stretching the maline, thumb tacks are used to fasten the maline to the wooden block. The maline, usually four to six thicknesses the required size, is pulled over the crown and a tack pushed in at the front, back, and sides at the base of the crown. One corner at a time, the material is steamed over a teakettle or steaming equipment, the fullness stretched out, and the maline caught to the block by more thumb tacks at intervals of not more than one inch. The maline must be allowed to dry thoroughly before removing it from the block. Then the lower edge is trimmed evenly and the crown mounted on a narrow, silk-covered crown band. A drape of flat maline folds may be used for the finish. The headsize band varies from one to two inches with the height and style of the crown.

3. Solid crowns with transparent maline brims. These crowns may have fitted maline brims, as described in section 1 of this chapter, or they may have brims of pleated, shirred, or corded maline.

Velvet crowns. Velvet crowns of any desired style that harmonizes with the shape of the brim may be used for a maline hat. Cap crowns, section tams, fitted tams, and saddle crowns are the styles generally used. A maline hat is ordinarily a dress hat, and the above-mentioned crowns, being soft, are more appropriate.

Fabric crowns. Taffeta, faille, satin, georgette, crêpe de chine, and moiré are most satisfactory fabrics to use for crowns on maline hats. Cap crowns, section and fitted tams, saddle crowns, and soft, corded, four-section crowns are the styles most used.

Flower crowns. Flower crowns on maline brims make lovely and colorful dress hats. Flat roses, rose petals, colored rose, or ivy foliage, and flat, small flowers make the most satisfactory crowns. Care must always be used not to select flowers of knobby or cup-like shape, as they will make the crown too heavy. A tied bow of velvet or ribbon is often added as a finish to this type of hat.

Straw crowns. Of the wide braids for hand sewing, fancy hair braids, elaborate visca-and-hair-combination braids, celophane, or satin straw are most suitable for crowns on maline brims. These are usually sewn in a soft semidraped form. They may be sewn in the hand or shaped over a wooden or buckram mold. Ordinarily only a low headsize of $1\frac{1}{2}$ or 2 inches is used for the foundation. The braid may be sewn in shape over a pressed crown, without stitching through the crown, and sewn to the brim. The top of the crown may then be cut out just before the hat is lined, leaving only a headsize band. A razor blade or sharp shears may be used for this. A smooth rather than jagged cut must be made so that the straw is not roughened.

Sewed crowns of milan, lisère, China split, milan hemp, and fine visca stripping are used for the maline hat in midsummer.

Lace

Lace transparent hats on wire frames are ordinarily made by putting the design or scallop edge on plain at the brim edge of the frame, extending the lace the width of its scallops or points and pulling the fullness up to the headsize in smooth fine pleats. The lace is more easily handled and the hat stays in shape longer if the frame is first covered with one thickness of maline. The crowns for lace hats are usually ordinary cap or puffed caps of lace with a silk or maline interlining.

1. **Metal lace.** Metal lace is used for transparent hats in either of two ways — as described in the paragraph preceding, or as all-over lace is used. (See page 106 of this chapter.)

The edge wire is often wound with velvet bias folds or narrow ribbon to match the crown or trimming in color.

2. **Valenciennes lace.** Val. lace is used in écru or pastel shades for children's transparent hats and in black for adults' hats. In both cases, the wire frame is first covered with maline or fine net. The lace is shirred or pleated and sewed to this foundation in ruffled rows.

The crown may be all-over lace, maline, organdie, velvet, or silk fabric. Val. lace is always more effective in écru or in pastel shades than in white. (See Chapter XIII, section I.)

3. **Lace flouncing.** Ordinary lace flouncing of three to five inches in width is used as directed in the beginning paragraph on page 104 under Lace.

It may be pleated in a fine No. 1 or No. 2 knife-pleating and sewed with the pleats stretched at the edge wire and crowded in close together, but flat at the headsize.

A wide flouncing may be pleated or shirred so that the one strip forms the entire brim and crown.

If pleated, the fullness is laid in closer pleat arrangement at the headsize.

In a shirred model, the shirring threads adjust the fullness to shape the crown. The crown may be shaped in this way over a pressed crown, or it may be shaped into a tam by using a group of shirrings at the top-crown center and one at the headsize.

If the lace scallop is used for the brim edge, it is necessary to work from the edge up to the crown center to adjust the lace to the frame irregularity of shape.

If a binding or flange is used for the edge, it is possible to work from the center-top crown down to the edge. Never try to gather all the fullness into the center-crown shirring in a small circle. Pull up this shirring to about two inches and sew the lace together in a folded, one-inch oval on this shirring.

4. All-over lace. All-over lace may be combined with other materials and fitted exactly as maline is fitted over a wire frame, or it may be treated as lace flouncing (see division 3, page 105).

LACE AND FABRIC COMBINATIONS

There are more lace hats made in combination with fabric than there are all-lace hats. The fabrics used and the methods of using them are the same as for maline hats. Milan-straw side crowns bound with silk are frequently used for summer lace hats. The top crown is lace over silk. The brim may be of maline with a drop over it made by extending lace flouncing beyond the frame edge.

GEORGETTE

Georgette is sometimes finely corded or shirred and used over a wire frame. It is seldom fitted plain unless fine straw or silk braid is used in an embroidery or braiding design over it.

II. PREPARING THE FRAME

Wire frames are used for transparent hats. For making see Chapter I.

WINDING WITH MALINE FOR BLACK AND WHITE HATS

For maline and lace hats, a matching color of wire is used and the edge wire wound with maline. This makes a nicer edge finish and gives a foundation on which to sew the lace.

In making a fitted maline hat or a hat of lace flouncing, brace wires show less and a smoother finish is obtained if they are not wrapped.

When making a fitted georgette or all-over lace hat, it is better to wind the brace wires. Only one thickness of lace and one of maline is used and only two thicknesses of georgette are used. Brace wires are less conspicuous when wound with fabric.

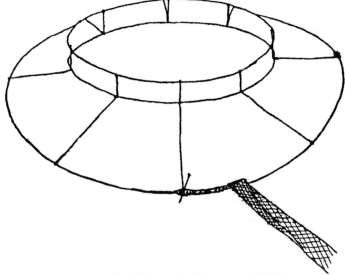

FIGURE 48. Winding a Wire Frame with Maline.

Cut a long, narrow strip of maline two inches wide. Fold it to three quarters of an inch. Pin one end to the edge (with the folded edge out) at a brace-wire intersection to keep the maline from slipping. Wrap the maline very tightly and smoothly around the edge wire, allowing the maline fold to lap only enough to cover its own raw edge.

When the wrapping is lapped too much it makes a thick, bulky edge. The edge wire must be covered, but must look thin and smooth. The maline strip may be pieced by fastening one edge with an overcasting stitch and starting another with the same stitch. All stitches must be hidden.

Dyeing to Match Metal or Colored Lace

Gasoline and oil paint may be used to dye any white silk wire any desired shade. The wire can be more easily handled before it is made into a frame than afterward. Yellow wire for use with gold-metal lace, and light gray for silver-metal lace, are not bad substitutes for metal paint.

Metallizing for Metal-Lace Hats

When using metal (gold or silver) lace the frame should match the lace in shade.

There are millinery preparations for the purpose which may be used on black or white wire.

The ordinary gold and silver paint used for steam radiators and picture frames may be purchased at any paint or wall-paper store. The frame should be made before the paint is applied. Apply this to the frame with a small brush. Black wire for a frame that is to be antique gold or silver, and white wire for a frame that is to be bright gold or silver, give best results.

III. EDGE FINISHES

In any hat, the edge finish is an important item.

In a transparent hat there are two important points to be kept in mind: (1) neatness of finish, (2) softness of line.

Braid Edges

On summer hats of maline, lace, and hair braid, a single row of plain, Swiss hair braid is often extended to give the effect of a maline fold.

Other hats use braid as a binding. Hair braid may form a binding but extend beyond the edge wire in a fold. Fancy celophane braids and fine milan braids are often used as edge finishes. When a wide braid is used, one row only is necessary and is used as a binding. Narrow braids have one row at the top brim and one at the facing edge. The edge wire of the frame wound with maline serves as a foundation to which the braid is sewn and shows between the two braids. This makes a thinner and more finished edge.

When a soft braid, as visca or satin straw, is used with maline, lace, or hair braid, it is often sewn to the frame edge (after the brim is covered) with embroidery thread in long stitches. This makes a soft finish.

Narrow braids may be sewn to the edge of a transparent hat to form a loop-fringe effect. The loops vary from $\frac{1}{2}$ inch (1 inch before looping) to 1 inch. The ends of each loop are cut. Several rows of the braid may be stitched together and used for a finish of loops over the edge of the brim. Visca, hemp, or milan stripping in the straw braids, soutache, ribbonzene, and chenille in the silk braids are good for this edge.

Ribbon Edges

Ribbon may be used very simply or very elaborately on the edge of transparent hats. It may form a simple binding stitched on with ribbonzene or silk floss.

It may be pleated or shirred and sewn in a design. It may be pleated and tied in a ruching and one row used at each facing edge (see Figure 73, page 141).

Hat patterns usually give directions for each hat.

A very good way to get new effects is to experiment with a buckram frame and a bolt of No. 3 or No. 5 ribbon. Fold the ribbon back and forth in irregular loops, or in points and squares until a satisfactory design is obtained. Then copy it on your hat.

Dovetail pleating makes nice edge effects on small, transparent hats.

FLANGES

Looking up the definition of flange in the dictionary will give any millinery student a good idea of what it means in millinery terminology and place it in her mind.

Do not confuse fold with flange. A fold on a brim edge either extends out from or over the edge wire on both sides, folds over, and is always double — a fold.

A hat may have a facing flange and a top-brim flange, but there is an edge division or cord or binding. It does not fold over the edge.

1. Velvet. Velvet is more used for flanges on transparent hats than any other material. It may be worn for winter and is invariably popular in summer.

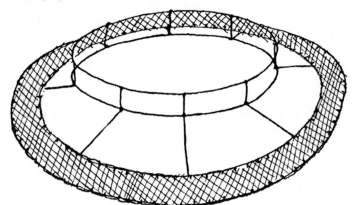

FIGURE 49. Flange Foundation for a Transparent Hat.

Flange foundation. A lightweight frame fabric under a flange keeps the frame-brace wires from showing through. A sprung-steel wire is used for the frame edge wire when a flange is to be used. A round brace wire should be tied on to the straight brace wires to make the desired flange width. Cut a circle (or fit a circular section) of crinoline, elastic net, or rice net, and buttonhole or blanket stitch it to the steel edge wire. Cut the net or crinoline on the inner brace wire and buttonhole it to the wire.

Process of putting on a flange. This same foundation may be used for a fold. Bind both wires with a one-inch bias strip of crinoline or mull binding. Put on the inner brim, which may be maline, lace, hair braid, georgette, net, or chiffon, and may be fitted, shirred, or corded. Sew the material to the inner flange edge and headsize before putting on the flange.

If the flange is one or one and one-half inches wide, a bias may be used to cover it. For a wider flange, a fitted section (cut as a brim is cut, but with the center cut out) is better to cover it.

Fit the flange whether bias or circular. Join the seams if a bias is used.

In fitting the bias, always bear in mind that the same bias length that fits the brim edge must lie smoothly on the inner flange edge. The tighter the material is stretched on the brim edge, the less fullness there will be to work out at the inner edge of the flange. Technically speaking, the smaller the fabric circumference can be made for the outer flange edge, the nearer it will equal the circumference of the inner flange edge. The bias is stretched over the large circumference and fullness pulled out at the smaller. (See Chapter VI, section IV, page 66, for flange measurements.)

Pin the material (bias or fitted) in place over the frame flange. Turn the outer edge over the frame edge and sew down as for any fitted brim. Work the inner edge over a wire for a finish or turn under a quarter-inch seam to be slip-stitched to the flange facing.

Fit the facing of the flange in the same way as the top. Finish both the outer and inner edges with a wire or with a slip-stitch.

2. Taffeta. Taffeta flanges are used on maline brims with maline crowns and with taffeta or flower crowns — also with lace and georgette brims and taffeta or flower crowns.

3. Maline. Maline flanges are used on all-over-lace brims, on shirred-lace brims, on fitted maline brims, and on hair-braid brims. They may be made over a silk foundation, or be transparent. When maline is used over silk, one thickness of silk is put on the frame first. Two or three thicknesses of maline are then cut and stretched over the silk flange. Ordinarily maline for a flange is cut on the straight, lengthwise. It may, however, be fitted without a seam.

For a transparent maline flange, the frame is prepared with a round brace to mark the flange width. Both brace and edge wire are first wound in maline. The edge wire should be of sprung steel as for fabric.

FIGURE 50. Maline Standing Fold and Velvet Flange on Hat of Taffeta.

Satin cable wire makes a nicer wire finish for maline than brace wire. The joining must be carefully made. Fit the wire to exactly the same size as the frame wire. Clip the ends evenly. Unwind the silk-wire wrapping, but do not cut it. Push back the cotton filler. Put on and clamp the joiner tight. Pull the cotton over it and rewind the silk. When the flange is finished the wire joining will not show.

IV. APPROPRIATE TRIMMINGS
LACE BOWS

Lace bows (and maline bows) are always attractive and becoming because they add two important things to a hat: (1) irregular width, (2) diffused lighting on the face. Any trimming which throws a heavy shadow on the face is ugly. Always select a fine, lightweight lace with a distinct design.

All-over lace or lace flouncing may be used. Single thicknesses, not loops, are best. Wire the edge of the bow with lace wire or a narrow ribbon wire. Cover the edge with a silk or maline fold slip-stitched over the wire or bind it with ribbon. Make a knot of the same material as the binding. Lace 12 × 10 inches with a shirring down the center makes a nicely proportioned bow. This gives two loops six inches long and ten inches wide. Bend the outer wired edge of the loops into pleats so that the loop does not flare too much. A bow this size may be used on small- or medium-brim hats and be posed at the back or front. Four loops may be used in place of two. (See Figure 51.)

FIGURE 51. Wired Lace Bow.

Dimensions are usually given with each hat pattern.

VELVET

Velvet is used on lace, maline, and metal hats. It is used in bands, bows, flowers, and rosettes.

On metal hats the velvet is often lined with metal cloth. For example, a silver-lace hat will have an Alsatian bow of French blue velvet lined in silver or blue metal cloth.

Black maline and lace hats for midsummer often have black velvet bows as trimming. These bows may be lined or have only inch-wide pasted hems for finish.

For this trimming a six-inch, bias, velvet strip (two widths of velvet) fifty inches long is pulled or draped around a crown and tied in a bow at the front or back or side. This is a trimming which is always conservative and satisfactory.

FLOWERS

Single roses, rose sprays, flower *cabochons* or rosettes, or wreaths of mixed flowers are the favorite flower trimming on transparent hats.

1. Silk. Silk flowers, such as beauty roses, rosebuds, violets, dahlias, and raisins are the main flowers under this heading. There are many silk fruits and unknown conventional flowers that are pretty on transparent hats.

2. Linen. The great majority of better flowers are of linen. Cowslips, forget-me-nots, grasses, wheats, fruits, heather, sweet peas, lilies, etc., come under this classification. These are most effective for formal, flat, *cabochon* arrangements and for mixed wreath sprays.

3. Metal. Metal flowers as related to transparent hats are, of course, used mainly on metal lace. Many of these flowers are mixed with silk and, though factory-made, give the effect of handmade flowers.

Grapes, apples, plums, and flat-petal flowers furnish most of the designs for metal flowers.

4. Velvet. Many of the better flowers in rose, pansy, nasturtium, fuchsia, and fruit designs are of velvet. These are expensive but of such exquisite coloring and fabric that they are well worth the expenditure.

5. Handmade. Handmade flowers are very satisfactory for many reasons. They furnish the most beautiful trimming, yet anyone who will take the trouble can make them at a small outlay for material. Colors may always be blended to give the desired color scheme. The really finished handmade flower is never common. Beautiful workmanship is the one thing that cheap manufacturers do not copy.

Georgette. Georgette is a good material for handmade flowers because it comes in attractive shades, has a soft finish, and is lightweight.

a. Over wire form. Twist three different-sized loops of tie wire, 2 inches for the smallest, $2\frac{3}{4}$ inches for the medium, and $3\frac{1}{2}$ inches for the largest. This means, take a length of tie wire and twist the ends together to form a loop.

Hold the wire loop in the left hand and pull georgette over the loop to cover it. Sew the georgette to the ends of the wire and cut off the fullness below the stitches. Make 4 small petals or loops, 6 medium, and 8 large ones. Assemble them into a daisy shape. Finish the center with a shirred puff of georgette.

Mount three small petals, one at the end and one on either side, evenly spaced, on a 3-inch cord and wind the cord with a georgette fold for stem and leaves.

Georgette, like silk, may be used for many other handmade flowers.

b. Shirred. One of the most attractive handmade trimmings is the georgette morning-glory shaped by shirring. A 10 × 4-inch strip of georgette is joined in a circle by seaming the 4-inch ends together. One end is shirred over a 7-inch circle of silk-covered cord (filled cord covered with crêpe or taffeta matching the georgette in color) or silk-covered ribbon wire. Starting just below this edge cording run silk shirrings $\frac{1}{4}$ inch apart. Pull up the thread while shirring to shape the georgette like a morning-glory. The fullness is pulled tighter until at the end the shirrings will be not more than $\frac{1}{2}$-inch in circumference. Mount the morning-glories on self-colored or green stems and leaves (see Figure 52).

Velvet. Velvet is used more in combination with other fabrics than in any other way. Pasted velvet flowers form the great exception.

a. Pasted. In making pasted flowers, paste large pieces of material together. Allow the cement or glue to dry thoroughly before cutting, so that the edges will not fray.

FIGURE 52.

Lilies (calla and tiger lilies), roses, pansies, and poppies are best adapted for this usage. Patterns are always furnished for the flowers with the hat patterns. Any clever girl can cut her own pattern from the actual flower or a drawing. Sharp scissors and a good quality of velvet are the main requisites in making these flowers.

b. Shirred. Shirred velvet is always prettier in colors than in black. Flat, oval, shirred-velvet flowers with cordings of contrasting color make rich trimmings when many shades are blended together.

For this, use velvet on the straight. Run fine shirrings $\frac{1}{4}$ inch apart. Pull up the first tightly to close the center. Sew the raw edges together in a flat seam on the wrong side. Pull up the shirrings until the flower cups very slightly. Cord or bind the edge in a contrasting color, using a bias strip.

The following are good proportions.

Strips $1\frac{1}{2}$ inches × 6 inches.
" 2 " × $7\frac{1}{2}$ "
" $2\frac{1}{2}$ " × 10 "
" 3 " × 11 "

c. Corded. One-inch bias strips of velvet may be corded on one edge with a draw string on the other, and the draw string pulled up to make the edge curve. Sew the shirred strip into a flat flower. Curve the end under in the same way that you start a braid crown center. These strips may be from six to ten inches long.

If the velvet is faced with a matching or contrasting color of silk, it may be curved into a conventional rose. Always curve the end down so that the cord starts from the center.

Silk. Many lovely handmade flowers are constructed from silk. The quality and shade of the silk used has a great deal to do with the success of the flower. The three important items are color, quality, and workmanship.

a. Pasted. Heavy silk is always necessary for this process. In pasting two thicknesses of fabric together, apply the millinery glue or cement lightly to each of the two surfaces. Then place them together and smooth out all wrinkles and air bubbles. Let the glue dry thoroughly before cutting the silk. Always paste the silk in the piece before cutting the flower (see Velvet Flowers, Pasted, in this chapter).

b. Shirred. Shirred-silk flowers have a wide variety of forms, from large roses and almost rosette-size stuffed flowers in vivid shades to small berries and forget-me-nots.

Shirrings help form the shades of many of these flowers.

Patterns and directions for making the flowers are always given with the hat patterns.

Shirred flowers are made from circles shirred and puffed, from shirred folds, from fringed strips shirred into various shapes, from two shades of silk cut in ovals and shirred and mounted on buckram foundations, and in a large variety of other ways.

c. Corded. Conventional morning-glories, trumpet flowers, and tulips are made from corded silk. One of the most effective of the large handmade roses is made of many petals of bias silk.

The bias strips have a tiny wire stitched inside a casing on one edge. The strip is cut into two- and three-inch lengths for the petals. The uncorded edge and the cut ends of the bias strip are shirred tightly to make the base of the petal. The stitching of the wired casing is entirely concealed by the roll. The petals are arranged in a rose shape and finished with a puffed center.

Rosettes

The idea of rosettes is centuries old, yet always there are new versions of it.

1. Maline. Maline rosettes may be shirred, looped, or pleated. Shirr a fold of maline 20 inches by 5 inches (20 × 10 before folding) over a 10-inch circle of silk-covered ribbon wire. Lap the ends 1 inch. Run shirrings below the ribbon wire at ½-inch intervals. Pull up the threads to shape the rosette. Sew the base of two such rosettes together. Pose them at the side or side back of a small-brim hat. The effect is pleasing because it gives irregular line, transparency, and an air of the unusual.

An effective maline rosette is made from the full width of maline tied with tie wire in loops over 2-inch flat lengths of frame wire. The loops are crushed close together, about 8 loops 2 inches long (4 inches doubled) without cutting the length. A long piece of tie wire binds the loops of maline close to the wire foundation. One maline loop is folded below the other as close as possible and held in place by a tight wrapping of tie wire. When complete, the maline is clipped all over to give a round, ball-like rosette. Two of these maline balls are posed at the side or front of a brim hat.

Pleatings of maline may be of double folds or of single maline with narrow braid or ribbon stitched on the edge. Side- (or knife-) pleating, box-pleating, and dove-tail pleating are made in long strips and mounted on circular or oval foundations of rice net or crinoline. These foundations should be covered with silk the same shade as the maline used.

2. Ribbon. Ribbon may be made into many, many different kinds of rosettes.

Narrow-ribbon loops, narrow-ribbon pleatings, points, and ruchings make tailored and semitailored rosettes.

Wide ribbons shirred, folded, and pleated form many different kinds of rosettes.

Two-inch loops of wide ribbon folded in a horizontal pleat and sewed in two rows around a 2-inch foundation form an effective and simple rosette. The center is finished with a flat double bow (four loops) and a wide knot.

For No. 100 to No. 150 ribbon the two ends should be joined in a circle and a group of shirrings $\frac{1}{2}$ inch apart run in one edge. These shirrings pulled up form the rosette center. The first shirring should be pulled up to 2 inches and folded flat and sewed in a 1-inch seam to make an oval center. The ribbon length varies from 16 to 24 inches for this kind of rosette.

The directions are always given on the hat pattern for all rosette trimmings.

3. Taffeta. Taffeta may be cut into petals and mounted in a rose-shaped rosette. Two shades of silk for this make an effective rosette. Black and jade, blush pink and rose, copenhagen and navy, brown and leather are good combinations.

Taffeta may be made into shirred rosettes like the ribbon rosettes described above. It may be corded and the cords pulled to shape the rosette. Hat patterns always give complete directions.

4. Velvet. Velvet rosettes may be made of a bias corner with shirrings and cordings, or from a plain bias shirred or corded, or from petals.

Many velvet bias rosettes are faced in silk or satin. The silk fabric may be a matching or contrasting shade. One rosette of satin soleil and one of velvet on a winter hat give good contrast of material.

Flower rosettes of velvet petals are very effective on a dress hat. These petals may be stitched and turned, or pasted and cut. In either case they are mounted on a foundation.

FEATHERS

Only the softer kinds of feathers are appropriate for transparent hats. Burnt peacock, natural ostrich, burnt ostrich, paradise, goura, and aigrettes are the feathers most often used.

QUESTIONS

1. Give directions for preparing
    a. A wire frame for a maline hat.
    b. A wire frame for a georgette fitted hat.
    c. A wire frame for a maline hat with a velvet flange.
2. How is a wire frame prepared for a metal-lace hat?
3. How are lace bows wired?
4. Are wire crowns often used on transparent brims? Why?
5. Make three kinds of handmade flowers in three different materials.
6. Cut patterns and make three different kinds of rosettes from tissue paper or from material.

CHAPTER X

DRAPED HATS

I. MATRONS' TURBANS
   Cutting of materials
   1. Materials
   Combination of materials
   Use of small brims
   Ways to obtain width
   Ways to obtain height
II. HAREM TURBANS
   Varied materials used
   1. Duvetyn
   2. Taffeta
   3. Satin
   4. Satin ribbon
   5. Tinsel cloths
   6. Brocades
   7. Straw cloth
   8. Maline
   9. Braids
   Cutting of materials
   Combinations of materials
   Frames used
III. DRAPED TAMS
   Patterns
   1. Sectional patterns
   2. Circular patterns
   3. Bias tams
   Trimming
   1. Machine embroidery
   2. Hand embroidery
   3. Beading

        General suggestions
           1. Points to remember for artistry
           2. Points to remember for becomingness
  IV. SECTION HATS
        Various section hats
           1. Two-section hats
           2. Four-section hats
           3. Six-section hats
           4. Eight-section hats
           5. Saddle-section hats
QUESTIONS

I. MATRONS' TURBANS

CUTTING OF MATERIALS

1. Materials. Materials used for matrons' draped hats are usually velvets, satin soleils, satins, duvetyns, heavy faille, taffeta, moiré silks, ribbon, straw cloths, and some straw and hair braids.

For *folded drapes* velvet, duvetyn, satin soleil, moiré satin, and straw cloth are good fabrics.

Hat braid and some visca and satin-straw braids are sewed into wide strips and used for folded drapes.

For *shirred, draped turbans* satin soleils, faille, moiré, and heavy taffetas are good fabrics. These fancy fabrics may be used for the shirred parts in combination with velvet, duvetyn, or satin braid for the fitted or unshirred part of the turban.

For shirring fabric may be straight, bias, or shaped. A pattern for the shape, or dimensions for cutting are always given on a hat pattern.

For *rosette effects* velvet, satin soleil, ribbon, taffeta, moiré, or faille may be used. These fabrics may be combined with other fabrics or straw braid or straw cloth.

DRAPED HATS

COMBINATION OF MATERIALS

Almost without exception a combination of materials with different finishes makes a more effective draped hat than a use of one material only. The materials may be of the same or contrasting colors. Below are listed a few good combinations for draped turbans:

Black velvet and black satin soleil.
Black velvet and king's-blue velvet.
Black soleil and copenhagen-blue velvet.
Brown soleil, brown velvet, and sand velvet.
Brown soleil and henna velvet.

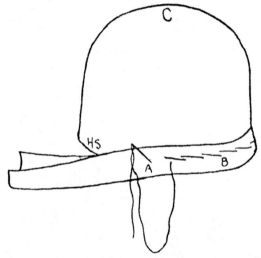

FIGURE 53. Making a Roll at the Headsize of the Crown for a Turban Foundation.

Black satin and black hair cloth.
Black moiré, copenhagen moiré, and black hair cloth.
King's-blue faille, black faille, and black hair cloth.
Plum satin, navy satin, and navy hair cloth.
Brown faille, sand faille, brown hair braid.
Navy taffeta, rose taffeta, navy straw cloth.

126   MILLINERY

Navy velvet, navy and gold brocade.
Brocade soleil, brocade and gold tinsel cloth.
Copenhagen-blue velvet and blue-and-silver-tinsel cloth.

Use of Small Brims

With very few exceptions, a small rolled or mushroom brim makes a draped turban much more becoming. Very few women past thirty years of age can stand a hard forehead line in a hat.

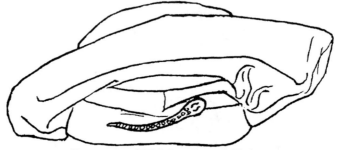

FIGURE 54. Width in a Draped Turban.

FIGURE 55. Fabric Turban Made of Bows Which Give Irregular Width.

FIGURE 56. Turban with Side Crown and Rosettes of Petals, Giving Width.

DRAPED HATS

Ways to Obtain Width

The placing of shirred rosettes or the side extension of shirred and folded drapes may be utilized to give soft width to a turban. This is especially necessary when the individual has high, wide

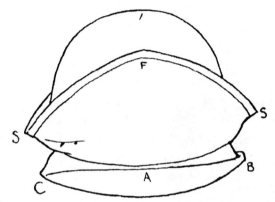

FIGURE 57. Frame Which Gives Height to Matron's Hat.

Note the high coronet *F* which holds up the drape. The brim *A* is rolled across the front and left side, line *C–B*. This roll to the brim and the coronet width at the sides, points *S*, make the perfect formula for a short woman with a full face oval.

cheek bones. Soft width in the hat gives better balance to the hat. Both drapes and rosettes may be held in place by wired braces.

Ways to Obtain Height

Where height is desired, rosettes and drapings may be extended above the frame crown and held in place by wired braces.

Feathers may add to the line of a drape and give further height.

II. HAREM TURBANS

Varied Materials Used

1. **Duvetyn** makes an admirable draped turban for street wear. The pile is deep, the colors are good, and the fabric becoming because it gives soft effects.

128 MILLINERY

2. **Taffeta**, either plain or embroidered, is an excellent fabric for a harem turban. It drapes well, comes in good costume colors, and is easily handled.

3. **Satin**, because of its high lustre, makes smart tailored hats. The body of good satin drapes well. Street shades are best.

4. **Satin ribbon** in street and dressier shades is well adapted for turbans. Because of the finished edges it is easily handled in combination with other materials.

5. **Tinsel cloths** make handsome harem turbans for dressy afternoon and evening wear for winter. Colors are good and the fabric well adapted for loosely folded drapes.

6. **Brocades** make good dress turbans for evening and formal afternoon wear. The colors and fabrics are lovely in contrast to the dark tones of fur wraps.

7. **Straw cloth** makes stylish turbans in combination with celophane or jet for early spring. A rhinestone pin gives a smart finish to an all-hair-cloth turban. A fabric headsize binding is usually necessary. Haircloth catches on to the hair and hair nets.

FIGURE 58. The Rolled Brim and High Rosette Trim Give Height and Lifted Line.

8. **Maline** makes smart dance turbans and turbans for summer-dress and street wear. Jet or rhinestone or fancy, col-

ored ornaments are the usual finish. The top may be transparent or may be of fabric.

9. **Braids** are sewn into wide stripping and usually combined with maline or fabric. A fabric headsize binding is necessary.

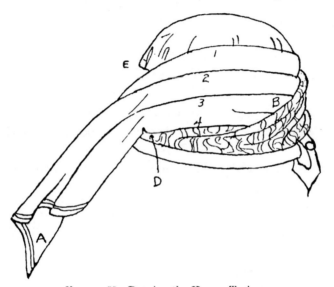

FIGURE 59. Draping the Harem Turban.

Points 1, 2, and 3 are folds in the bias drape. Point *A* shows the straight selvage edge. Point *B* shows the lap of the plain material under the brocade.

CUTTING OF MATERIALS

Fabrics are ordinarily cut on the bias for draping. Usually a circular section is used for the top of a harem turban. The drape ends may be pulled in at the headsize or folded under one another. For all straw and maline drapes the latter method is better. All headsize materials should be smooth in finish. Maline and ribbons are, of course, always used on the straight.

Combinations of Materials

Combinations of material make good dressy effects. A few combinations are listed below.

Black satin, black and silver brocade.
Copenhagen, jade, and rust faille.
Gold, jade, sapphire, rust, and henna maline.
Black maline and black satin.
Brown maline and brown satin.
Brown maline and brown and gold tinsel cloth.
Jade maline and jade and silver tinsel cloth.
Copenhagen and silver brocade and copenhagen and silver tinsel.
Copenhagen and silver brocade and copenhagen velvet.
Jade velvet and Chinese embroidery.
Black soleil and Chinese embroidery.
Brown soleil and brown satin and Chinese embroidery.

Frames Used

Turban frames, pressed or made of bias elastic net, or soft crowns with headsize bindings are used for the usual harem turbans. Soft crowns with tiny brims and soft crowns with coronets and small brims make becoming variations in frame shapes.

III. DRAPED TAMS

Patterns

Patterns are always given for the shape of draped tams.

1. Sectional patterns always give the method of assembling the sections and for applying any design given.

Four-section, draped tams are usually made without any frame other than a soft, pressed crown. These make good flapper hats and good foundations for embroidery.

DRAPED HATS

Six-section, draped hats are made without frames. They are adapted to embroidery and come in youthful and in older designs.

Eight-section tams are made sometimes on crowns, sometimes without any frame. They are usually of fabric, though ribbon and straw cloth are used occasionally.

2. **Circular patterns** are used for many embroidery fabrics and straw-cloth tams. Usually they are beaded, braided, or embroidered.

3. **Bias tams** are of velvet, taffeta, or crêpe and usually have some width added in an extra drape or bow.

FIGURE 60. High Drape Tam with Small Headsize, Brim, and Some Width.

TRIMMING

Almost all tam trimming is some sort of appliquéd flat design. A few quills, feathers, and pins are used.

1. **Machine embroidery** has been made a fine art. In the larger cities beautiful machine embroidery is done by professional workers. These places will furnish designs or use those provided by the customers.

2. **Hand embroidery** can be beautifully done by the home milliner. It requires only careful work following the designs given on the patterns.

Ribbonzene comes in lovely, soft colors and is used to make entire designs and in combination with yarn, embroidery floss, tinsel threads, or chenille.

Silk embroidery threads occasionally make an entire design, but are generally used in combination with something else.

Appliqué embroidery makes beautiful effects. Patterns for this work are always given with the hat patterns.

Yarn embroidery is used on fabric and straw cloth. It is often used in combination with straw stripping, chenille, and ribbonzene.

FIGURE 61. Tam Which May Be Braided by Machine or Embroidered by Hand.

3. **Beading** is an effective trimming for this type of hat.

Wooden beads often outline appliqué. They come in lovely colors and are best used in combination with tinsel, yarn, ribbonzene, or embroidery floss.

Bugle beads are used in black, silver, gold, and colors on dressy tams, usually in combination with silk floss or tinsel threads.

Nail heads are used in white, black, and colors. They are most effective when used in solid designs or in combination with bugle beads or embroidery threads.

GENERAL SUGGESTIONS

1. **Points to remember for artistry** in draping tams, are:

Symmetry of folds. Folds should always be smooth in line, never puckered or tight. The general line of the folds should slant in the same or directly opposite directions.

Tacking of drape. The stitches used for tacking must always be hidden. They may be tie tacks or the tacking may be done from inside the crown using small stitches on the outside and long ones inside the crown.

Always use the fewest possible number of stitches to secure the drape.

Color harmony. Always be careful to choose harmonious colors for embroidery colors that blend well. Vivid colors may be used for the tam fabric and dull colors for the embroidery or the reverse. Never use vivid embroidery colors on a very vivid fabric, or dull embroidery colors on dull fabrics.

Self-tone embroidery should be used if a dull effect is desired.

2. Points to remember for becomingness. Draped tams furnish one of the most becoming types of hats. The drape may be adjusted to give becoming lines for different kinds of faces. Always try on and readjust the drape to suit the individual. This makes an excellent class problem.

Harmony of line. Becomingness depends greatly upon the degree to which lines of the hat harmonize with one's physical lines.

a. Harmony of line with facial contour. The tam must be draped so as to preserve a balanced proportion.

A small face must never have a too-heavy drape.

A long face oval needs soft width without length draping.

A wide face oval takes proportionately wide draping.

b. The mode of hairdressing has a great deal to do with the becomingness of hats. A large knot of hair in the back needs always to have some brim and some drape in the back and at the sides. A plain mode of hairdressing needs some brim and a soft drape. A soft, full mode of hairdressing can stand plainer and more severe lines in a hat.

c. Harmony with costumes. A draped hat must harmonize in style and fabric with the costume it is designed for. A draped hat may be worn for street or dress, according to the fabric used. Evening fabrics for evening wear, street fabrics for street wear is the rule.

IV. SECTION HATS

Section hats are hats which receive their form from the fitting together of shaped pieces, or sections, of material. The majority of these hats are made in pie- or wedge-shaped sections, the apex of the sections forming the top center of the crown. Two-section crowns (see Figure 31, page 79), six-section crowns (see Figure 32), and saddle-section crowns (see Figure 24) are notable exceptions.

Patterns are given for the shapes of section hats.

Various Sectional Hats

1. **Two-section hats** usually have a crown or no frame at all; they are used for misses and children, being delightfully soft.

2. **Four-section hats** are made sometimes on a crown, sometimes on a crown and brim. Any embroidery or design used is always given with the pattern. See Figure 103 for section hat with crown and brim foundation.

3. **Six-section hats** are made with or without brim foundation. A crown or headsize band is always used. A pin, tassel, or ornament is often the only finish. The material is usually fabric. Any embroidery design is always given on the pattern.

4. **Eight-section hats** have the same characteristics as six-section hats (see above).

5. **Saddle-section hats** are very smart for both dress and street wear. Embroidery or handmade flowers are the usual trimming. Patterns are always given for any handwork.

QUESTIONS

1. How are materials cut for a matron's draped turban?
2. What materials are used for harem turbans?
3. Is a harem turban a dress or a street hat?

DRAPED HATS

4. Give some fabric combinations for matron turbans and harem turbans.
5. How should a straw turban be finished at the headsize?
6. What foundation is used for
    a. A circular tam?
    b. A section tam?
    c. An eight-section hat?
    d. A two-section hat?
7. How are wooden beads used to the best advantage?
8. What frame has a two-section hat?
9. How should a draped tam be draped for an individual?
10. What is an evening draped tam?

CHAPTER XI

TAILORED TRIMMINGS

I. SEVERE, FACTORY-TAILORED HATS
II. SEMITAILORED HATS
   General street wear
   Sport wear
III. KINDS OF TAILORED TRIMMINGS
   Ribbon
      1. Band and bow
      2. Flat ornaments of pleating and loops
      3. Tied and pleated ornaments
      4. Pleating
   Braiding
      1. Soutache
      2. Ribbonzene
      3. Tubing
   Cording
      1. Small, silk-finished cords
      2. Large, silk-finished cords
      3. Unfinished cords
      4. To make a finished cord
   Ornaments
      1. Pins
      2. Buckles
      3. Medallions
      4. Braid ornaments
   Feathers
      1. Wing
      2. Goura
      3. Numidy

4. Coq
5. Hackle
6. Vulture
7. Burnt and glycerined feathers

QUESTIONS

Tailored trimmings may be divided into two classes according to the kinds of hats they trim.

I. SEVERE, FACTORY-TAILORED HATS

Severe, factory-tailored hats are hats made ready to wear and are invariably trimmed with a band and bow of grosgrain ribbon like a man's hat. A Knox sailor is a good example of this type of hat.

II. SEMITAILORED HATS

These hold more interest for the milliner and millinery student because they are largely made by hand.

GENERAL STREET WEAR

Many of the hats for general and street wear come under this heading. Tailored and semitailored hats of velvet fabric, straw, and braid-straw cloth come in this class.

With the present-day styles, the better hats of this type are soft. Stiff hats do not accord with the fashions favored in the mode of hairdressing or in frocks and coats.

SPORT WEAR

Hats for sport wear may be, and usually are, made very simply, depending on design, line, and color for their style, but to be comfortable they must be soft and lightweight.

Fabrics, such as taffeta and duvetyn, ribbons, soft braid, and felts are suitable materials for use in making sport hats.

III. KINDS OF TAILORED TRIMMINGS

Ribbon

Ribbons have been used for decorative purposes since the days of Queen Elizabeth. At that time they were worn by both men

FIGURE 62. Hat with Ribbon Ornament Sewn on a Shaped Foundation Which Is Used to Trim a Small Mushroom Hat.

FIGURE 63. Showing the Same Sort of Ornament as in Figure 62 with Different Pleatings and a Different Hat.

and women of high rank. Ribbons were used for garters and shoe roses by the elegant women and men of high degree. Ladies used ribbons for their exaggerated styles of headgear and to adorn their dresses with bows, rosettes, and lover's knots.

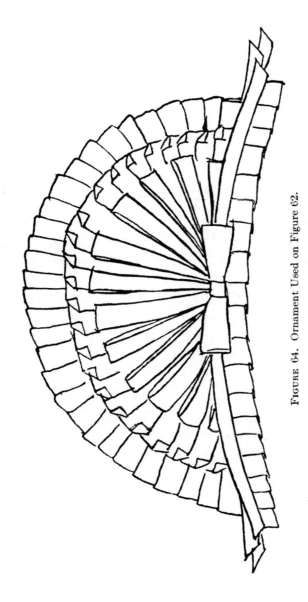

FIGURE 64. Ornament Used on Figure 62.

140   MILLINERY

For tailored trimmings there is no other one article which holds so unique a place. It may form the simplest trimming,

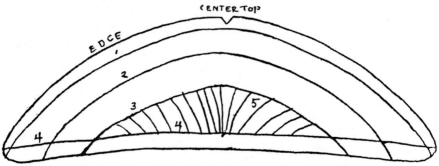

FIGURE 65. Buckram Foundation for the Ornament with Lines 1, 2, and 3 for the Ribbon Pleatings and Lines 4 and 5 for the Center Loops.

or be used for the most elaborate of the tailored designs. It very rightly comes first in the list of tailored trimmings.

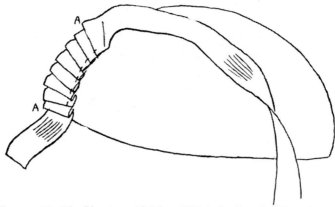

FIGURE 66. The Pleatings of Ribbon Which Outline the Edge, Line A.

1. Band and bow. Many tailored and sport hats have merely a band and bow of ribbon as trimming. Many embroidered hats have a band and bow of narrow ribbon as a finish.

TAILORED TRIMMINGS 141

2. **Flat ornaments of pleating and loops.** This type of ornament is made on a foundation of elastic net, crinoline, or buckram.

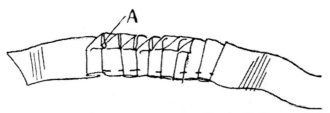

FIGURE 67. For the Second Row of Ribbon the Pleating Is Sewn and the Corners Turned before Fastening It to the Ornament.

In most cases the foundation is wired and covered with silk or fabric to match the ribbon.

Half-moons, triangles, ovals, and semicircles make good foundation shapes. The edge of the foundation may be outlined with loops of one inch or less and filled into the center with flat pleatings. To turn back one corner of the pleats makes variety in the combination of straight lines and crosslines. In this sort of ornament the center is finished with a flat bow of two or more loops and two or more ends. A flat cluster of loops and ends is often used to add length or width to an ornament (see illustration 64).

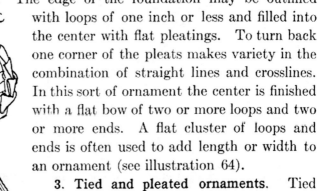

FIGURE 68. Tied and Pleated Ornament.

3. **Tied and pleated ornaments.** Tied and pleated ornaments are always circular in shape, never square nor elongated. This is because they are formed of loops tied on a central thread as an axis (see illustration). Each loop is really the radius of a circle.

The number of loops used for these ornaments varies with the size of the finished ornament and the width of the ribbon.

142   MILLINERY

For No. 6 ribbon, 18 to 20 loops 2½ inches long are used.

For No. 9 ribbon, 14 to 16 loops 2½ inches long are used, or 18 loops 3 inches wide.

Explicit directions are always given with each different ornament featured on any pattern (such, for instance, as Figure 74).

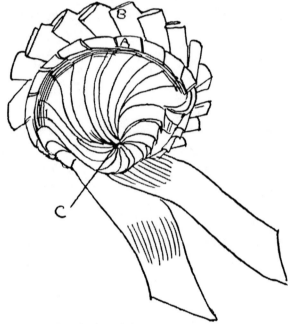

FIGURE 69. Tied and Pleated Ornament Turned at a Different Angle.

4. Pleating. Pleating has many different uses on the tailored hat.

Ribbon is often sewed into bands or strips of plain, knife-pleating and used *as finishes for brim edges and crowns* (see Figure 73).

Very narrow ribbons, No. 1½ or No. 2, are used in pleated bands *to outline sectional-crown seams or brim sections.*

TAILORED TRIMMINGS 143

Fine ribbon pleatings are used *as pipings with which to join straw braid* as it is sewed to brim and crown.

No. 6, No. 5, and No. 3 ribbons are pleated flat, sewn down the center, and the loops tied (see illustration) to make pleating to be

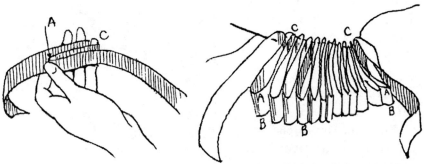

FIGURE 70. Folding of Loops with Thumb and Small Finger as a Measure.

FIGURE 71. Threading the Loops on Heavy Thread.
This thread is pulled up and tied in a hard knot to form center *C*.

used *in designs*. These pleatings may outline appliqué flowers or beaded motifs, or may form an individual design which is filled in with beads or tinsel-thread stitching (see Figure 75).

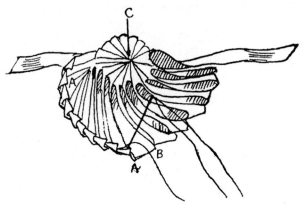

FIGURE 72. Turning Back the Corners of the Ribbon Loops.

Wider ribbons are box-pleated in double or triple pleats and tied. Such pleatings are used for designs in the facings of rolled brims.

Taffeta may be cut in straight strips to resemble ribbon and fringed on both longitudinal edges. When pleated, this fringing makes lovely edges on large hats, or entire brims for small hats.

Shot silk, that is, changeable silk, is effective when treated in this manner.

Several different shades may be used, as a row of French blue, one of beige, and one of almond-green taffeta on a brown satin hat. The pleating should be sewn close together to give a soft, thick effect.

FIGURE 73. Completed Hat with Ribbon Pleating Used for Brim Edge, Crown Band, and Ornament at Right Side.

BRAIDING

1. Soutache. Soutache is always an effective braid to use for both conventional and floral designs.

It is often used in a loop or a wigwag, all-over design to cover entire brims and crowns.

Sewed in loops on a brim edge it makes a soft and flattering finish like an uncut fringe.

This idea is stressed by several of the French designers who use loop bands of soutache to outline tricorns and make cockades.

2. Ribbonzene. Ribbonzene is used for fringe, for fancy

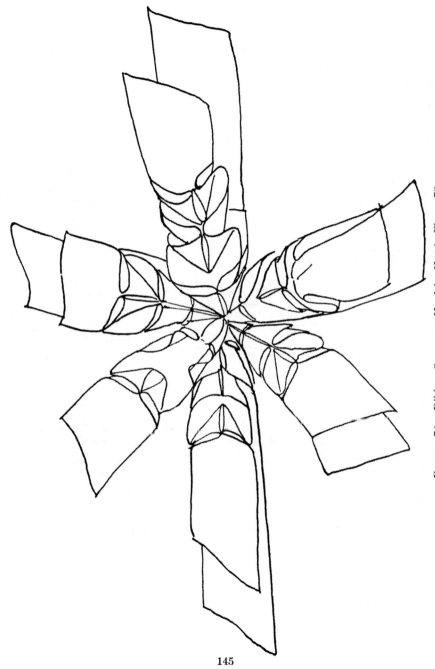

FIGURE 74. Ribbon Ornament Used for Hat in Figure 73.

146 MILLINERY

braid weaving, and for many embroidery designs. It is wonderfully effective when used to couch chenille or heavy yarn and for an all-over, honeycomb design (see Figure 93, page 163).

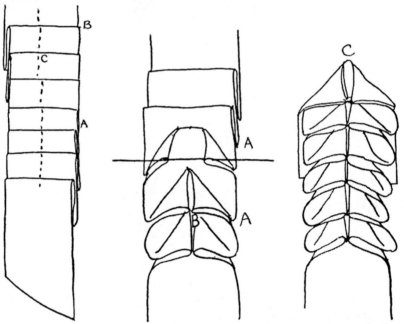

FIGURE 75. Pleating Sewed down the Center with Small Stitches.

FIGURE 76. Tying the Pleats with a Silk Thread Tie-Tack Stitch.

FIGURE 77. Showing the Finished Banding.

3. **Tubing.** Tubing is used in much the same way as soutache.

Straw tubing comes in visca and hair. Both of these tubings are used on maline hats, on hair hats, and on taffeta, satin, and straw-cloth hats. They may be used in design or in an all-over wigwag or loop pattern for entire hats.

Silk tubing is used on straw-cloth, on fabric, and on hair-braid

TAILORED TRIMMINGS 147

hats. It is used, too, for fancy woven or loop edges on mushroom or rolled brims.

CORDING

Cording is much used for finishes. It is always used easily because it can be made of the same fabric as the hat and so be in perfect harmony.

Cording is always made by covering a cord with a bias strip of fabric.

1. Small, silk-finished cords. These cords have the two bias edges of the covering turned inside and the two fold edges thus formed slip-stitched together.

Ornaments. Circles, irregular triangles, crescents, and shaped forms are covered solidly with finished cords covered in satin

FIGURE 78. Feather Stem Finished with Cord.

or silk to match the hat. These ornaments make good-looking finishes for feathers and hats that have corded edges.

Edges and flanges. Brim edges and flanges are often outlined with finished cords in a self or contrasting color.

When cords are used the edges of the hat or flange are basted, and the cords sewn over them as a finish.

Finishes. Finished cords may be used to wrap the stems of feathers, such as ostrich, aigrettes, or quills.

A circle of finished cording is often used to finish a rosette center, a shirred top crown, or a wing.

Many designers and trimmers go by the rule — "When in doubt use finished cording."

Finished cords make neat finishes for pleated ruffles, shaped flanges (as scalloped flanges), flower edges, and maline folds.

In fact, a well-made cord adds to the finished effect of a hat in almost any capacity in which it is used.

2. Large, silk-finished cords. These are usually made on a filled-wool cord which is very light in weight and may not be covered with a mull casing.

These large, finished cords are often made by measuring the bias width of material needed, stitching the casing the correct size, and drawing the cord through the casing (see illustration).

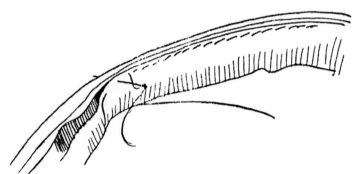

FIGURE 79. Unfinished Cord Used to Join Seams. Shown from the Wrong Side.

Fancy edges may be made by interlacing cords in loose scallops for large, mushroom brims. Small brims are effective when these large cords are twisted or braided to make the edge.

Ornaments. Two or more shades of cord may be sewn on a circular or shaped foundation to make trimming for sport and tailored hats.

TAILORED TRIMMINGS 149

Brims. Entire brims are made by sewing large, curved cords together. These are shaped over pressed frames just as in braid sewing (see Chapter VIII). A cord ¾ or ½ inch in diameter is shaped in circular rows which are slip-stitched together.

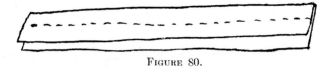

FIGURE 80.

3. Unfinished cords. Unfinished cords are used in at least half of all the hats made.

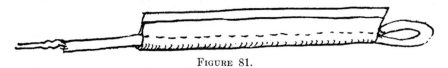

FIGURE 81.

Seams Seams for section crowns, tam crowns, cap crowns, in fact, most crowns, are effective when joined together with a cord. (See Chapter IV, section II.)

FIGURE 82.

Edge finishes. In place of a wire edge finish, an unfinished cord may outline the brim edge and the facing be slip-stitched to it.

Where a bias or fitted brim is extended beyond the frame to make a soft edge, the two facings are usually joined together with a cord finish.

Always be careful to take the seam up close to the cord. If a space is left between cord and seam it makes an unsightly finish.

4. To make a finished cord :

(1) Cut a bias strip of material. Stitch a casing the size of the cord to be used. Stitch this separately in the hand or by machine — not on the cord (Figure 80).

FIGURE 83.

(2) Fasten one end of the cord to a hairpin, or bodkin, and run it through the casing (Figure 80). Fasten the end of the cord to the end of the casing (see Figure 81).

(3) Pull the cord through to turn the casing right side out (see Figure 82).

(4) Run the cord through the finished casing (see Figure 83).

ORNAMENTS

Ornaments make an effective finish and decoration for many tailored and semitailored hats.

1. Pins. Pins may be of rhinestone, crystal, enamel, pearl, jet, or composition.

A pin should be so placed as to stress the line and design of the hat.

A pin (fancy) is to a hat what a period is to a sentence.

2. Buckles. Buckles are used when colonial designs are popular. They finish drapes or ribbon bows. Most buckles are made of silver, cut steel, jet, rhinestone, or a celluloid composition. There are many variations of shape and design.

3. Medallions. Medallions are usually of foreign make with clever workmanship and design in metal, mother of pearl, and

TAILORED TRIMMINGS

various compositions. They are used as finishes in much the same way as fancy pins.

4. Braid ornaments. Braid ornaments are much used on cheaper hats.

Silk. Silk ornaments are of fancy, colored braids, of bias-silk folds, and of silk cords.

Tinsel. Tinsel ornaments are much in favor some seasons and out of style other seasons. Gold and silver braid are sewed in various designs or wound on different kinds of molds. At present these are mostly used on cheap hats.

Straw. Straw of fancy weaves and textures is much used for ornaments on straw hats of the factory type.

Composition. Ornaments of fancy shapes and designs such as women's heads, King Tut designs, and floral motifs, are used as finishes for small, draped hats.

Feathers

Feathers play a large part in trimming the tailored hat. It always pays to buy a good feather and to use it many times, rather than to buy a cheap feather. A cheap feather makes a poor appearance to begin with and, of course, looks worse every time it is worn.

1. Wings. The use of wings varies with the styles in vogue. There is no other trimming which has the clipped smartness of wings. Most of them are made of chicken or sparrow feathers glued or sewed on a wired foundation.

2. Goura. Goura is a dainty, graceful feather very effective when used in quantity, but very expensive. The cause of its high cost is easily understood when you see the tiny spray which grows on the topknot of the goura bird. It is naturally gray and white, but as a rule, the feathers are dyed to match the hat.

3. Numidy. Numidy feathers have a straight stem and a very long, drooping fiber. Usually they are used in clusters and in a standing trim like aigrettes. They are an African importation.

4. Coq. Coq in black, in iridescent shades, and in colors, is used to trim many smart hats. Spanish coq feathers are iridescent, long, and curved. They are the tail feathers of the Spanish rooster.

Usually they are used to trim fall and winter hats. They are a little heavy-looking for summer wear.

5. Hackle. Hackle feathers are finer than the feathers used for wings. They are the soft and shiny feathers that grow on the neck of a fowl.

Dyed and mounted, one would never guess their humble origin.

Paradise sprays often have dyed hackle at their base to hide the stems.

Entire turbans, many fancies, and many bands are made of dyed hackle.

6. Vulture. Vulture has only recently come into use. It makes beautiful fancies, bands, and ornaments. The fiber is shorter than ostrich; the stems are long and pliable. Vulture fancies are as handsome as aigrettes, much less cruel in origin, and more durable and less expensive.

7. Burnt and glycerined feathers. Much of the fine feather work done today has been made possible by the glycerine processes, which burn the fuzz or fiber off the common fowl feathers. This leaves the fine, aigrette-like centers of the feather.

Burnt goose. Many handsome bands and fancy ornaments are made of goose feathers which have been subjected to a glycerine process.

These feathers are usually mounted on a crinoline foundation, as they are short.

TAILORED TRIMMINGS

Glycerined ostrich. When ostrich has been glycerined, the feathers are much finer and thinner looking, and are used in quantity.

Entire facings are made of narrow, glycerined ostrich sewed in rows. For this, secondary ostrich stock is used.

Glycerined peacock. Glycerined peacock has much the appearance of Numidy. Many very handsome feathers are made of peacock which has been glycerined and dyed.

The old superstition of the bad luck attendant on peacock feathers is likely to pass away. Many people are wearing them without knowing it.

QUESTIONS

1. What are the essential qualities of a sport hat?
2. Make three different ornaments of pleating and loops, using ribbon or strips of paper.
3. Give four uses of pleatings.
4. How is soutache used on tailored hats; ribbonzene; tubing?
5. How is finished cording made on fine cords; on large cords?
6. Give three uses of small finished cords.
7. Give three uses of large finished cords.
8. What is the important point to remember in cording seams?
9. Are cheap feathers a good investment?
10. What are hackle feathers; glycerined feathers; goura feathers; what feathers are generally used for wing construction?

CHAPTER XII

DRESS-HAT TRIMMINGS

I. TRIMMINGS FOR WHICH THE HAT IS A BACKGROUND
   Flowers for the garden hat
   Elaborate ostrich trimmings
   Paradise
   Burnt goose
   1. Bands
   2. Fancies
   3. Entire crowns
   Elaborate coq
   1. Bands
   2. Fancies
   3. Crowns
II. TRIMMING WHICH IS PART OF THE DESIGN
   Flowers
   1. Single flower
   2. Sprays of flowers
   Feathers
   1. Ostrich heads
   2. Paradise
   3. Aigrettes
   4. Fancies made of ostrich fiber
   Embroideries
   1. Silk floss
   2. Appliqué materials in design
   3. Ribbonzene
   4. Tinsel thread
   5. Tinsel-ribbon embroidery
   6. Tinted ribbon
   QUESTIONS

DRESS-HAT TRIMMINGS

In choosing a dress hat remember always that there are two outstanding qualities for which designers strive in making this type of millinery. One is beauty, the other, style or *chic*. To attain both is a rarity. Decide in your own mind whether you want a sweet hat or a smart hat. Have both qualities when it is possible. Be sure that you know in your own mind what you want. You are then a great deal more likely to attain it.

Dress-hat trimming may be divided into two classes, trimming which uses the hat for a background only, and trimming which is part of the design.

I. TRIMMING FOR WHICH THE HAT IS A BACKGROUND

There are times when a hat must be chosen for the trimming, rather than the trimming for the hat. Such trimmings are:

FLOWERS FOR THE GARDEN HAT

Flower manufacturing has reached a high degree of perfection within the last ten years. Morning-glories, nasturtiums, fuchsias, sweet peas, camelias, dahlias, wistaria, and hosts of other flowers are copied with absolute fidelity to form and color.

Not content with following the colors used by nature, the designers and dye makers go further and give us blue roses and pink lilies-of-the-valley. These are often so artistic in their conception and so satisfactory

FIGURE 84. Straw Garden Hat with Wreath Trimming and Crepe Underfacing.

in effect that the divergence from authentic coloring is not objectionable.

Many beautiful wreaths and sprays may be purchased ready-made, but the same effects may be obtained at much less cost when a little taste and care is used in the making of a wreath.

Colors and flowers chosen to match or harmonize with hat and frock make a much more pleasing completed costume than can be had in a combination wreath which is made of flowers and colors selected at random.

FIGURE 85. Garden Hat with Front Trimming of French Flowers.

There is no more picturesque hat for wear with organdie, lace, and linen frocks than the garden hat. Large, floppy, straw-body hats laden with flowers lend color and atmosphere to summer costumes.

These body hats may be purchased untrimmed in any good department or millinery store. Facings or bindings of georgette, organdie, velvet, or taffeta make a more finished-looking hat and give an opportunity for the use of color.

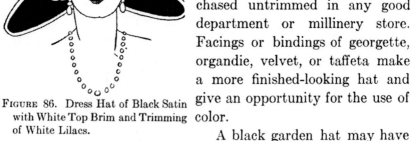

FIGURE 86. Dress Hat of Black Satin with White Top Brim and Trimming of White Lilacs.

A black garden hat may have a wreath of buttercups, green, yellow, and blue wheat, yellow and blue berries, and green and rose apples. If the wreath is tied

DRESS-HAT TRIMMINGS

with dull blue ribbon and the hat faced in either green, blue, or rose, it may be worn with almost any costume. It is lovely worn with any one of its own colors.

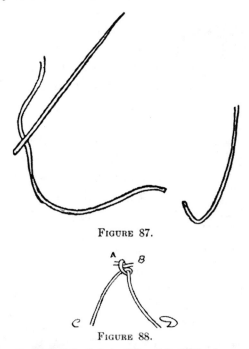

FIGURE 87.

FIGURE 88.

Figures 87 and 88 show the detail of the tie-tack stitch used for tacking flowers and feathers. Stems are sewn with ordinary stitches. The sprays and feathers are caught loosely with a tie-tack stitch.

If you watch flower coloring you will see that almost any, or all, colors in the spectrum may be combined if they are used in the correct shades and proportions.

ELABORATE OSTRICH TRIMMINGS

When a hat is to be made with an elaborate ostrich trimming it is easier to adapt the hat to the ostrich than vice versa. This does not mean ostrich heads or quills or plain bands, for they may

158   MILLINERY

be adapted to a hat; but the more elaborate ostrich bands and crowns. These come in a variety of shapes, styles, and colors.

FIGURE 89. Hat Designed to Fit the Ostrich Trimming.

When they are used, the designer tries the feathers on various frames, and if none is completely harmonious, shapes a frame to make it a fitting background for the feathers as well as becoming to the individual.

PARADISE

Paradise and aigrettes are the most beautiful of all feathers but they are procured in a manner so barbaric that it is inconceivable that any well-bred woman would want them.

Since there is no accounting for tastes, their use must be given space. These feathers are so elaborate in themselves that ordinarily a plain hat with style of line is the best to use for them (see Figure 90).

For aigrettes, a draped turban with smooth, smart lines, or an irregular turned-up brim of soft lines is the best background. These shapes are becoming to most people.

For paradise birds (which in themselves are showy but not pretty or artistic), a large-brim hat is necessary.

Sprays of paradise feathers, without a head, are as beautiful as their

FIGURE 90. Hat Designed for Trimming of Aigrettes.

source is cruel. Our feminine vanity and love of the beautiful, together with a faculty for shutting our eyes to the disagreeable, is what has kept them on the market.

Paradise sprays may be used on small or medium-large rolled-brim hats, tiny sailors, and turbans.

Burnt Goose

Burnt goose comes in a variety of elaborate forms.

1. **Bands** are shaped in circles for the edges of mushroom or upturned brims. It is seldom that a frame exactly fits such a band. The band may be slashed and lapped slightly or the frame may be cut to fit the band.

Other bands are really frames in themselves and need only have edge folds, crowns, and facings added to have finished hats.

Figure 91. Hat Designed in Rust Faille for a Band of Dull Henna Aigrettes.

2. **Fancies.** Burnt-goose fancies are made on shaped forms to give aigrette-like effects.

Small brims, irregular, medium-sized brims, and a variety of large brims and turbans are used as background for these feathers.

3. **Entire crowns** of burnt goose give a variety of lovely effects. These come already made in a variety of shapes and colors. Brims of straw cloth, satin, velvet, or taffeta are used to mount these crowns.

Elaborate Coq

Coq makes very handsome small hats for girls and matrons, and dignified, handsome, brim hats for matrons.

1. Bands. Bands of coq are for side crowns only. The feathers are too long for brim bands except where other feathers are used for the edge.

2. Fancies. Coq fancies are much favored by the French designers and make smart, small hats. A small hat with an elaborate use of coq is very smart, if not pretty, and highly suited for what is called a dressy street hat.

3. Crowns. Crowns of coq are made on plain molds for turbans and on small brims for matron hats.

For more elaborate dress hats these crowns come with long coq tails attached at side or back, or with smaller coq fancies at the side or front.

II. TRIMMING WHICH IS PART OF THE DESIGN

This is the type of trimming used for ninety per cent of the hats of today.

Ten or fifteen years ago most of the hats worn were factory made (often of fine quality) of straw or velvet. All that the milliner needed to do was to sew on trimming, which might be elaborate or simple, according to the quality and quantity desired.

Today most of the design of the hat is in the making. Trimming is only a small part of the design.

Flowers

1. Single flowers. Single flowers are used as a finish to dress and semidress hats.

Rose. Roses are often so beautifully made that to use just one is artistic perfection. A single rose may be posed at the side of a soft tam crown; it may be used on the edge of a shirred fold on a large brim; it may catch in the velvet or fabric drape of a matron's turban; be caught to the bandeau of a Watteau hat; or be nestled in the lace facing of a baby's hat.

Gardenia. Gardenias are conventional in shape and appropriate for the more or less severe midsummer hats of taffeta and hair. A gardenia at the side of a soft crown or at the right-side front of a brim edge is both smart and pretty.

Handmade flower. The handmade flower is essentially a part of the design of fabric and straw hats. Most of the good-looking handmade flowers for hats are flat. Large handmade flowers are for dresses, not millinery. Patterns and directions for making are always given with the hat pattern.

FIGURE 92. Handmade Spray on a Large Dress Hat.

2. Sprays of flowers. Sprays of flowers may be used around a top crown; around a side crown; across the back of a brim; on the facing of an upturned brim; at the headsize of a brim which is turned up in the back; or on the brim of a large dress hat (see Figure 92).

Rose sprays. These are usually of small roses or of a mixture of a few large and a number of small roses. Midwinter dress hats and spring and summer straw and hair hats are frequently trimmed with rose sprays. Leghorn and roses seem always a happy summer combination.

Facings usually match frocks and roses in color.

Mixed sprays. The better flowers which are made into mixed sprays usually have one or more large flowers in the center and a spray of smaller flowers extending out on each side. The large flowers serve as balance to the arrangement and to hide the stem ends of smaller flowers.

In making these sprays, assemble two small sprays which are a pair. Cut the extra stem ends off. Join the ends of the two sprays together and fasten the larger flowers, or flower, over the joining.

Metallic flowers. Metallic flowers are used to trim late fall and early winter dress hats of velvet brocade, satin, and tinsel cloth. These come already arranged in sprays.

More elaborate sprays may be made like the mixed sprays, as directed in the paragraph above. Grapes, roses, berries, and small flowers are used with a few thistles, roses, poppies, and unknown flowers.

Handmade sprays and wreaths. Handmade flowers may be used for either sprays or wreaths.

Instead of being made into wreaths or sprays and sewed onto the hat, they are sewed onto the hat separately in a wreath foundation. This is because extra stemming, such as ready-made flowers have, would make the hat heavy and give extra work which has no value. Patterns and directions for handmade sprays and wreaths are given on all hat patterns where they are used.

Feathers

Feathers are often used on dress hats to give point to the design of the hat.

1. Ostrich heads. Ostrich heads, correctly posed, may be made the most sophisticated finish for the design of a dress hat. An ostrich head is the head or tip end of a full ostrich plume.

Rain-proof finishes have been so perfected that ostrich feathers are now more satisfactory than ever.

Blended shades of ostrich used on a velvet hat of two tones is artistically satisfying.

For example, a Gainsborough hat may be of violet velvet faced in wistaria and trimmed in two ostrich heads the fibers of which are dyed blue and wistaria.

There is no more artistic trim for the large, black hat than clustered ostrich heads; not huge, sweeping, willow plumes, but graceful, nodding ostrich heads.

2. Paradise. Small sprays of paradise may droop gracefully from the folds of a draped turban to give a wide, soft frame for the face.

FIGURE 93. Design Showing Appliqué of Fabric and Honeycomb Design of Ribbonzene.

In a picture hat they accentuate the sweeping line of a wide brim.

In a medium brim with curves they have all the grace of the old cavaliers' hats.

3. Aigrettes. Aigrettes make the finishing trim on draped and semidraped hats of velvet, satin, hair, haircloth, tinsel cloth, and brocade.

The hats may be turbans or have large or medium brims.

4. Fancies made of ostrich fiber, as:

Bands. Ostrich is sewed and glued onto shaped bands to make trimming for dress hats. These come in bow shapes, in crescent shapes to fit into the curve of a brim, and in rosette shapes.

FIGURE 94.

Figure 94 shows the stitches for honeycomb all-over embroidery.

Flowers. Ostrich flowers are usually round in shape, giving a morning-glory or rose effect. They make soft, unusual trimming finishes for the large hats of exaggerated shape and style.

Embroideries

Embroidery of every sort has been, and is still very popular for dress hats. It is fundamentally part of the design of the hat. Entire crowns and entire facings are solidly embroidered.

1. **Silk floss.** Embroidery floss is seldom used alone to make the embroidery on a hat. It is used in combination with nail heads, bugle beads, wooden beads, chenille, tinsel thread, or ribbonzene.

2. **Appliqué materials in design.** Appliqué in elaborate designs of conventional lines in Chinese-embroidery motifs or in intricate, all-over patterns makes handsome dress hats.

FIGURE 95. Chinese Embroidery in an Appliquéd Design on the Front of a Turban.

Duvetyn and suède cloth, velvet, broadcloth, and heavy silks are used for this. The edges are finished with couching or blanket stitching of embroidery floss, yarn, or tinsel.

Beaver cloth is used in appliqué design on felt hats. The edge is caught down with yarn, chenille, or beads in harmonizing color.

166   MILLINERY

3. Ribbonzene. Ribbonzene is used alone in honeycomb, all-over designs and in combination with crêpe folds, tinsel braid, chenille, yarn, and floss.

FIGURE 96. Appliqués Cut from Vari-colored Velvet for a Straw Hat.

FIGURE 97. Cut-out Design from Printed Silk for a Fabric Hat.

4. Tinsel thread. Tinsel embroidery thread imparts richness of color as well as design. It is rarely used alone but combined

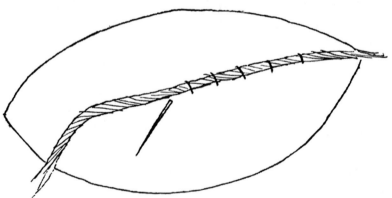

FIGURE 98. The Couching Embroidery Stitch Used for Much of the Appliqué Embroidery.

A heavier floss, ribbonzene, or yarn is couched on the appliqué edge with a floss thread.

with floss, ribbonzene, Chinese embroidery, medallions, Chinese gold twist, tinsel ribbon, or beads.

5. Tinsel-ribbon embroidery. Tinsel ribbons are made in lovely designs of solid tinsel and in combination with colored silk or fiber.

These ribbons laid flat on the hat and caught at curve or turn by tinsel thread make rich and lovely effects.

Solid turbans and facings are embroidered in conventional line and flower designs of these ribbons.

6. Tinted ribbon. Ribbon woven with plain or scalloped edges and tinted in two or more shades makes lovely floral designs.

An easy method is to cut a conventional rose stencil, mark the pattern on the hat, and outline and fill in to the center with shirred rows of tinted ribbon.

QUESTIONS

1. How are the two major divisions of dress-hat trimmings made?
2. Give the uses for and types named of ostrich trimming.
3. Make two sprays of handmade flowers.
4. Make two wreaths of artificial flowers. It is a good idea for this to be done in connection with the lesson on cleaning and dyeing. Old flowers or cheap new flowers may be used.
5. How is a hat designed for an elaborate feather band or brim?
6. Name two admirable trimmings for matrons' hats.
7. How may a garden hat be made to blend artistically with many dresses?
8. How is tinsel ribbon used in embroidery?
9. How is appliqué embroidery finished?
10. What are the best appliqué materials?
11. Make two doll hats with original embroidery design.
12. What is the evil, if any, of using aigrettes?

Note to instructor: This may be made an educative point because women are largely unconscious of their part in the aigrette industry.

CHAPTER XIII

CLEANING AND REMODELING

I. CLEANING
    Leghorns
        1. Rye-bread process
        2. Wall-paper-cleaner process
        3. Soap-and-water process
    Milans
        1. Dyed milans
        2. Natural milans
    Panamas
        1. Wall-paper-cleaner process
        2. Rye-bread process
    Straw braid
        1. Wall-paper-cleaner process
        2. Cleaning fluid
        3. Soap-and-water process
        4. Pressing braid
    Flowers
        1. Cleaning fluid
        2. Dyeing
        3. Pressing
    Feathers
        1. Ostrich
        2. Aigrettes
    Lace
        1. Washing
        2. Tinting
    Felts
        1. Cleaning fluids
        2. Art gum
        3. Fuller's earth

Velvets
    1. Cleaning fluid
    2. Refinishing
II. REMODELING
Pressed hats
    1. Cutting
    2. Edge finishes
QUESTIONS

I. CLEANING

LEGHORNS

Materials of good quality stand remodeling better than cheaper ones. This holds true of all materials under all processes.

A good leghorn may be cleaned, pressed, and reused many times. It is advisable never to let a leghorn hat get very dirty, but to clean it frequently.

Cleaning processes **1** and **2** may be used without taking the trimming from the hat.

1. Rye-bread process. To keep a fine leghorn hat in good condition clean it for every ten times it is worn.

Cut about four inches from the end of a day-old loaf of rye bread. Hold the end of the loaf in the right hand and scrub the hat with the cut end. The gummy texture of the bread rubs off the dust as you scrub. When all dust has been removed, brush the hat with a good, stiff brush.

2. Wall-paper-cleaner process. When a hat is very much soiled and you do not want to rip it, purchase any good wall-paper cleaner. Apply it as for wall paper. Brush thoroughly with a stiff brush.

3. Soap-and-water process. When a leghorn is very much soiled and is to be remodeled, rip all trimmings and facings and brush thoroughly.

Stretch the crown over a wooden block which is the shape that you want it to be when dry. A stiff buckram crown may be used.

Fasten the brim down to the table with thumb tacks at intervals of two inches around the edge. Place about six tacks around through the center of the brim.

Use a suds made of Ivory Soap Flakes. Apply with a brush that has short, stiff bristles. Scrub well. Rinse with a brush and clean water.

Wipe as dry as possible with a soft, absorbent cloth. Allow it to dry thoroughly.

Before removing the hat from the block, take the tacks from the brim. Press brim and crown with a moderately hot iron. Use a thickness of mull or crinoline over the leghorn so that the iron cannot scorch it.

For reshaping see section II of this chapter.

Milans

1. Dyed milans. A dyed milan may be cleaned by wiping it with a cloth of the same color dipped in ammonia solution.

2. Natural milans. To clean a natural-colored milan, have ready a sauce dish or deep, small container with a rounded tablespoon of sulphur and a lemon cut in half. Dip the cut end of the lemon in the sulphur, pressing it down until a considerable amount of sulphur is absorbed by the lemon juice.

Rub the milan well with this lemon. When the sulphur is rubbed off into the straw, dip the lemon into the container again. When the entire hat has been covered with the sulphur-lemon solution allow it to stand one hour. Then brush the hat well with a very stiff brush.

Oxalic-acid process. In using oxalic acid for cleaning straw dilute the acid with water using a half and half solution.

Wipe off the acid with a soft cloth which has been dipped in weak ammonia.

Panamas

1. **Wall-paper-cleaner process.** (See section I.)
2. **Rye-bread process.** (See section I.)

Straw Braid

1. **Wall-paper-cleaner process.** Straw braid may be cleaned, either on the hat or ripped from the hat, by following directions given on any good wall-paper cleaner.

2. **Cleaning fluid.** Dip a soft cloth, the color of the straw braid to be cleaned, into the cleaning fluid, and wipe the braid thoroughly with it.

3. **Soap-and-water process.** A good quality of straw braid may be scrubbed with a brush which has been dipped in an Ivory Soap Flakes solution. Rinse in clear, warm water. Shake partially dry. Wrap in newspaper. Allow it to stand for one hour, and press.

4. **Pressing braids.** Always press straw braid on the wrong side with a moderately hot iron. Too hot an iron will stick to the straw. Too much water will tend to run the braid strands together.

Flowers

Often good flowers are only dusty, not faded. These can be reused if they are cleaned. Flowers that have a good shape, but are faded, may be dyed a new color. Flowers that are only crumpled may be pressed and made to look like new.

1. **Cleaning fluid.** Flowers can be washed with a cleaning fluid which drys rapidly. Dip them in the cleaner (gasoline may be used) and rub with a soft brush. Shake them dry.

2. Dyeing. If the flowers to be dyed are soiled, they should first be cleaned in gasoline.

For the tinting, mix oil paint with gasoline and dip the flowers in the solution. Always try one flower first to get the shade.

Lovely effects are obtained by using two shades. For example, if faded white lilacs are to be tinted, dip them first in a soft blue solution. Let this dry. Dip just the tips in a dark rose or dull red solution. An infinite variety of lovely effects may be obtained in this way.

Calcimine (ordinary dry calcimine used for walls) may be mixed with gasoline and used to dye flowers.

3. Pressing. If flowers are only crumpled they may be freshened by pressing each petal and leaf with a moderately hot iron. Place the flower flat on the ironing board and, starting with the center petals, work to the outer edge.

Small flowers may be crushed flat, when they are crumpled, to form a flower facing or to be used for a turban. Put a moderately hot iron on top of the flower and let it stand for two minutes.

Feathers

Any really good feathers may be cleaned and reused many times. Pasted wings and feathers may be protected by maline when they are first put on a hat. They are never very satisfactorily remodeled once they are blown.

1. Ostrich.

Cleaning fluid. To clean ostrich prepare two deep bowls. In the first make a suds of cleaner, such as gasoline, and Ivory Soap Flakes. In the second put clear gasoline.

Wash the ostrich in the first bowl. Wash and rub it thoroughly just as though you were shampooing it. Rinse all the soap out in the second bowl. Shake the ostrich dry.

CLEANING AND REMODELING

The tips may then be curled slightly, although at present most ostrich is used straight.

Curling process. The best method for the amateur to use for curling ostrich is the heat method. Heat gives a soft curl just as moisture straightens the ostrich fronds. Hold the plumes over a low-burning gas flame, in the smoke from burning sugar, or over a hot steam radiator. Sugar placed in an iron skillet and allowed to burn sends up a heavy smoke which is admirably adapted for the purpose.

Always try a few ostrich fronds to test the force of the heat lest it burn the ostrich.

A novice is apt to break the fiber if she uses a curling knife.

2. Aigrettes. In handling aigrettes, be careful not to break the center stem or quill.

Soap and water. The process given is for white aigrettes. Colored ones may be washed in the same way. They, of course, do not need whitening.

Have ready two deep, medium-sized bowls; in one make a strong solution of Ivory Soap Flakes and lukewarm water. In the second put clear, lukewarm water.

Shampoo the feathers well in the soapy water. Rinse thoroughly in the clear water. Shake out all the loose drops of water. Roll the feathers in a bath towel. Let them stand ten minutes.

Whitener. Place a quantity of cornstarch in a flat, long box or on a large plate. Shake the feathers until the fibers begin to loosen up and fluff out. Then roll them in cornstarch. Shake the feathers until dry, rolling them frequently in the starch.

LACE

Almost any kind of lace may be cleaned and reused.

1. Washing. Any silk, linen, or cotton lace may be washed.

Soap-and-water process. White, cream, or écru lace may be washed with any good, white soap. The soap must be thoroughly rinsed out. Wrap the lace in a towel. Wring it as dry as possible. Press with a moderately hot iron.

Cleaning-fluid process. Colored laces may be washed in cleaning fluid and soap, and rinsed in clear cleaning fluid. Shake almost dry and press on the wrong side with a moderately hot iron.

Pressing. Black and dark laces often need only be shaken well and pressed with a hot iron.

2. Tinting. Very cheap laces may be made to look quite unusual by tinting them. Valenciennes (val.) lace, ruffling, and all-over lace take on a very different appearance when they become soft écru, dull blue, or rose. Mix ordinary calcimine with water. Dip the lace, shake it partially dry, and press on the wrong side.

Felts

Light felts can be kept in good condition only if they are cleaned frequently. Never allow them to get really soiled.

1. Cleaning fluid. Dip a soft cloth in cleaning fluid, rub it over the felt with the nap. Brush the felt dry with a soft, clean brush.

2. Art gum. Art gum will remove spots or streaks from felt when they are not made by a liquid. Coal soot, pencil marks, or dust are easily removed by rubbing art gum over the felt.

3. Fuller's earth. Cover the felt with a thick coat of fuller's earth. Wrap a dry cloth around it and let it stand overnight. Brush all the earth out with a stiff hat brush.

Velvets

Velvets, like any other fabric, should not be allowed to get very much soiled. Better results are obtained when they are cleaned frequently.

1. **Cleaning fluid.** Dip a soft cloth (a piece of the same material as that being cleaned is always preferable) in cleaning fluid and rub it lightly over the velvet. Much light rubbing will not mar the velvet, though pressure will mar it very easily.

2. **Refinishing.** Velvet may be given a new finish and an entirely different appearance in either of two ways.

Mirroring. This process is really only sponging and pressing. A very hot iron and much sponging are necessary. Always run the iron with the nap of the velvet.

Pull all threads from the velvet. Place it flat on the board. Sponge all over with a very wet cloth rubbed over the surface with the nap. Press with a hot iron. Run the iron lightly over the velvet first. Press down with more weight the second time. Responge and press until the velvet has a smooth and shining surface.

Crushed finish. To make crushed velvet, clean it first (see above). Then dip in clear water for only an instant. The velvet should be just barely wet, not soaked. Wring loosely and shake. Hang it over a line to dry. This gives a crushed effect which is very pretty. Crushed velvets are used for draped hats and for fitted hats in combination with plain materials.

Pressed Hats

1. **Cutting.** Pressed hats, both straw and felt, may often be cut and reshaped to look like new. If the shape needs to be changed at the headsize, it is best to rip or cut the crown from the brim.

Crowns. Old crowns may be raised to make them higher by cutting them and setting in a piece of buckram.

They may be cut and lapped to make the headsize smaller. A soft crown is usually draped over the left side. Slash the crown up $1\frac{1}{2}$ inches at the left. Lap a seam and sew it flat. If the headsize is still too large, slash and lap the side crown, where the seam will be covered by the hat trimming.

Brims. Pressed hat brims may be cut and reshaped just as pressed frame brims are cut (see Chapter II, section I).

2. Edge finishes. The cut-brim edges in most cases need to be rewired (as a frame edge is wired). This wire must be covered. There are several methods to choose from.

Fabric folds. The edge may be finished with a bias fold of silk, satin, or velvet. These folds may be finished with an embroidery stitch; they may be slip-stitched on both edges; or the fabric may be worked over a wire.

Ribbon binding. Narrow grosgrain or fancy ribbons stretched over the edge make a good, tailored finish. The edges may be slip-stitched down or sewed with long, embroidery-thread stitches.

Fancy-straw braids may be sewed over the edge of straw brims.

Chenille or yarn braids are effective for felt hats. These braids may be caught down with embroidery silk, yarn, chenille, or ribbonzene, or they may be sewn with a slip-stitch.

Blanket-stitch edges. For sport hats both straws and felts may have the edge wire covered by a blanket stitch of heavy yarn, chenille, or ribbonzene.

QUESTIONS

1. Give two processes for cleaning leghorn hats; three for cleaning felts.
2. Give detailed steps in cleaning a milan.
3. Why is it better to clean a hat frequently?
4. Give two ways of remodeling flowers.
5. What is the rye-bread process?
6. How may ostrich feathers be cleaned?
7. How is velvet mirrored?
8. What soap is best for millinery cleaning processes?
9. Give three uses of calcimine.
10. How are cut-brim edges finished in remodeled body hats?

CHAPTER XIV

COLOR HARMONY AS APPLIED TO THE INDIVIDUAL

   I. Purpose of Color in Adorning the Person
  II. Color *versus* Temperament
 III. Chart of Color Combinations Suitable to Various Types
Questions

I. PURPOSE OF COLOR IN ADORNING THE PERSON

The purpose of all personal adornment is to enhance the beauty of the individual.

Garments are worn by wax models in a shop window to show the garments, not the models. She who wears her clothes to show them puts herself in the same relative position as the inanimate model.

This does not mean that garments need not be smart, need not be beautiful — but the contrary. Who can know that a girl with olive skin, clear brown eyes, smooth brown hair is beautiful with a quaint and subtle charm of her own if she adopts the fads of the moment regardless of her own difference from other people? If she frizzes her hair and wears the blue, coral, and jades appropriate for a vivacious blond, her own charm is lost. She becomes merely one more like all the rest.

By choosing garments and styles that are in themselves attractive, regardless of their suitability, many girls who could be immensely attractive are merely second-rate editions of what they might be.

Uniformity may be desirable for an army or a penitentiary;

certainly it is necessary for the manufacturing of automobile parts or electrical appliances or tooth pastes. But no feminine being has any desire so to submerge herself in the masses.

The girl described should wear soft blue-greens, green-blues (pottery shades), Quaker gray, black with some oyster white, ivory or jade in relief, and some of the flame shades. Imagine this girl in a soft gray crêpe or organdie gown with exaggerated collar and cuffs of écru organdie in John Alden style, and a black brim hat of shepherdess lines with tea-rose facing. The effect is such as to make you see the girl as an interesting person of outstanding individuality. Smooth, shining hair and quaint collar attract one to the face of the wearer. Tea-rose flush brings out the color needed to make the pallor of an olive skin beautiful. Rich black velvet with long, plain lines, square neck, and a touch of jade in earrings or pendant, and a hat of black with irregular, soft lines makes her a portrait of distinct beauty.

A study of potential values in the appearance of an individual is the greatest asset in successful dressing of the individual. Color is one of the greatest helps in this matter of bringing out all the possibilities of beauty.

The first principle to remember in choosing colors for an individual is that you are working for just one thing — the glorification or beautifying of that person.

The beauty of a given color or color combination or garment is nonessential if it does not improve the looks of the person who is to wear it. An artist blends colors that they may give full value to each other. He uses colors complementary to one another, as a green with yellow tones with yellow for blending, or an orange-yellow with a blue-green for contrast. Each color is considered in relation to the other for the effect desired.

In dressing a woman, every color must be considered in relation to the effect desired, but it must be remembered that the desired color effect is essentially different from that worked for in mere color harmony. The color combinations must be harmonious both in themselves and as applied to the wearer.

The foundational element in all human beauty is an effect of health. An unhealthy person is never beautiful. A healthy-looking person is never quite ugly, whatever her features or coloring may be.

The desirable colors for milady's hat are those that give her the rosy glow of health. The obvious answer to this demand is rose, red, or pink. The less obvious is certain blues for certain types, certain greens, tans, browns, and black for others. There is also the infrequent exception of the girl with too much color.

II. COLOR *VERSUS* TEMPERAMENT

Webster defines temperament as " the peculiar physical and mental character of an individual." It is because temperament includes two elements, physical and mental, that color *versus* the temperament of an individual becomes a matter of complication.

One's physical and mental individuality do not always match. Many a misshapen scrubwoman has the soul of a poet and is kindness itself. Too often the girl with limpid, violet eyes and rose-petal skin is the most soulless, selfish, and empty-headed of people.

Why not dress the body in colors that will enhance the expression of one's temperament? It is just as stupid to dress your body in ugly clothes as it is to fill your mind with cheap and ugly literature.

We are more than small who laugh when the apparently stolid and uninteresting person blossoms forth in gay and unseemly colors. But not all of us who love color have been taught the value of restraint and repression. Nor have all of us enough kindness to look for values underneath ugly exteriors. And since the Golden Age is not yet in sight and people not apt to be more patient and kindly, it behooves us to improve our externals and our own values as measured in the casual contacts of every-day life. Casual contacts are quite apt to shape our entire destiny in a work-a-day world.

Not even a fat woman need be uninteresting and unpleasant in appearance, and no one (except a diseased person) need be actually obese.

We say that a girl is handsome or homely according to whether or not her features and her physical person conform to accepted standards. Irregularity of features, however, need not keep one from being interesting, unusual, attractive, and popular. Study *your* set of features and *your* kind of body and make a fitting setting for them. If you have a gay and adventurous soul, give humanity some hint of it in your outer wrappings. In all casual or momentary meetings, we have the same status as package goods. No one is interested in a package of sweetmeats mussily and carelessly wrapped, if sweetmeats are to be had done up carefully and neatly.

Many girls with inward charm of person and intellect feel bitterly aggrieved because girls with more apparent but superficial charm attract attention. Such girls must learn to pay more attention to the outward expression of their inherent attractions. This work-a-day world is busy with the obvious, the well-advertized. If the girl of retiring personality, of hidden depths of feeling and character, can learn to reveal and accentuate these qualities, she stands a far better chance of success in life than does the girl of flashing but shallow appeal.

QUESTIONS

1. What is the purpose of color in adorning the person?
2. Should clothing be expressive of ourselves as we are, or as we should be?
3. Plan three costumes with hats which you consider suitable to your individuality.
4. Give three color schemes suitable for street wear for
    a. The golden blond.
    b. The clear brunette.
    c. The mixed brunette.
5. In what fundamental way does the clothing of a wax model differ from that of an individual?

III. CHART OF COLOR COMBINATIONS SUITABLE TO VARIOUS TYPES

	Rose	Flame and Poppy Shades	Orange and Bittersweet Shades	Fuchsia and Amethyst Shades	Purple	Orchid	Pink	Jade Green, Peacock, Olive	Nile and Reseda Green	Chinese and King's Blue
Brunette Types										
Clear Brunette	★	★		★						
Olive Brunette			★					★		
Mixed Brunette	★						★	★		★
Blond Types										
Clear Blond		★			★	★	★	★		★
Golden Blond			★		★			★		
Olive Blond										
Mixed Types		★		★		★	★			★
Red-haired Types										
Titians			★					★	★	
Chestnut	★		★					★		
Golden			★			★		★	★	
Green-eyed						★		★	★	

CHART OF COLOR COMBINATIONS SUITABLE TO VARIOUS TYPES—*Continued*

	French Blue	Navy Blue	Golden Yellow, Canary, Marigold, Buttercup, Goldenglow	Greenish Yellow, Chartreuse, Citron (Dead Leaf Green)	Taupe, Battleship, Mole	Beige, Sand, and Barley	Golden Brown, Tobacco, Cocoa, and Leather	Dark Brown, Negro, and Seal	Black	Copenhagen and Tapestry Blue
Brunette Types										
Clear Brunette		★	★	★	★					★
Olive Brunette		★				★	★			★
Mixed Brunette	★		★				★	★	★	
Blond Types										
Clear Blond	★	★	★			★	★	★	★	★
Golden Blond	★	★					★		★	★
Olive Blond	★	★								★
Mixed Types				★	★	★	★	★	★	★
Red-haired Types										
Titians	★		★			★	★		★	
Chestnut	★	★	★		★	★	★	★	★	
Golden		★	★			★	★	★		★
Green-eyed		★	★			★		★	★	

CHAPTER XV

LINE HARMONY

I. FUNDAMENTAL PRINCIPLES OF LINE
   Principles of line in art
      1. Sculpture
      2. Painting
      3. Japanese prints
   Principles of line in millinery
      1. General principles
      2. Harmonizing of line with the costume
      3. Harmonizing of hat lines with the general style
II. PRINCIPLES OF LINE AS APPLIED TO THE INDIVIDUAL
   Objects to be obtained
      1. Greater beauty for the individual
      2. Beauty of line in the hat
      3. Conformity with fashion dictates
   Specific types
      1. Prominent nose
      2. Small or snub nose
      3. Wide face oval
      4. Narrow face oval
      5. The round face
   Mode of hairdressing as adapted to types
      1. As it affects the facial contour
      2. As it affects the profile
      3. As it affects the hat
  QUESTIONS

I. FUNDAMENTAL PRINCIPLES OF LINE

Anyone who studies algebra and geometry develops the imagination and trains the eye to see. The really successful hat is one which has style, line, good workmanship, and becomingness.

The first three attributes involve mathematics and it takes all three to make the fourth — becomingness.

Principles of Line in Art

The fine arts are those which have primarily to do with imagination and taste, and are applied to the production of what is beautiful. Sculpture, painting, and architecture are the accepted fine arts.

1. Sculpture. Sculpture is the representation of life in wood, stone, or metal.

Millinery more nearly approaches sculpture than it does any other of the arts in the matter of line. Each has the three dimensions; each involves the breaking up of mass into line and form, though methods, materials, and purpose are vastly different.

Greek sculpture attained the highest point of perfection and is universally accepted as the standard of beauty. Simplicity and fidelity of line are the keynote of Greek masterpieces in bronze and marble. Every superfluous line is eliminated. Beauty, grace, and naturalness are the result.

Marble pictures made with the utmost simplicity of line and detail attain the highest point in the sculptor's art.

2. Painting. Webster's definition of painting is "a work of art in which objects are presented in color on a flat surface."

The painter may use light, shadow, and color, as well as line. He may utilize all four to give the illusion of form and dimension to a flat surface. The great painting is that one which gives the illusion of reality, the effect of life and form, with a few, telling lines. Art involves constant practice in restraint and elimination. A few lines, bold and decided, or fine and delicate, give beauty which cannot be produced by mere detail.

3. Japanese prints. Japanese art is an outstanding example of what may be accomplished with line. Japanese prints stand alone for sheer beauty in this regard.

Principles of Line in Millinery

1. General principles. In millinery, line gives to the hat that intangible thing called style. A hat may be very pretty and becoming, but have no line or style. In choosing a hat it is always well to know which you want.

2. Harmonizing of line with the costume. It must be remembered that a hat is but one unit of a costume. To make a complete and perfect whole, the line of the hat must be in harmony with the general lines of the rest of the costume.

A hat of tailored lines may be all that is desirable when worn with street costumes and utterly ugly when worn with frocks.

3. Harmonizing of hat lines with the general style.

Mode of hairdressing. The mode of hairdressing is always a determining factor in the matter of becoming line. A fluffy mode, a smooth, severe arrangement, a shingle, or a Russian bob make the lines of the head entirely different. The lines of the hat must be adjusted and adapted to each manner of dressing the hair. Different qualities are required in a hat to make it comfortable. This changes the line of the crown, and the brim line must be changed to correspond.

Fashion silhouette. Styles in line change with the seasons. What is good this year, may be out of fashion next.

II. Principles of Line as Applied to the Individual

Objects to Be Attained

The modern idea of facial beauty is regularity of features and profile with irregularity of head line — the head line being exaggerated by the knot or cut of the hair. This idea does not vary greatly from the ancient Greek sculptor's formula.

The classifications given and the hat lines suggested are all done with the purpose of gaining an effect of regularity of features. Every woman knows that there is no real beauty or depth of character in a perfectly regular face. Few of us need worry over our perfections. But all of us like to make our faulty features less conspicuous so that we are not known as " that girl with the long nose," or " that girl with no chin."

1. Greater beauty for the individual. As has been said, the real purpose of any hat is to add to and enhance the good points of the wearer.

2. Beauty of line in the hat. Beauty of line in the hat is the goal for which the designer strives. The choosing of that hat with good lines, which brings out and complements the good and minimizes the bad points of the individual, is the task of the milliner.

3. Conformity with fashion dictates. In selecting a hat it is necessary to choose one in keeping with the lines of the rest of the wardrobe — sport lines for sport clothes; dressier, softer lines with dressier suits and frocks. Close, trim hats are best for the narrow silhouette and straight lines. Larger hats or medium hats of exaggerated lines are in keeping with the bouffante silhouette. High bandeaux and raised back lines are in keeping with the Directoire profile.

Always, in line, as in other matters of dress, the paramount thing is to have such harmony that the clothing is but a fitting frame for the pictured individual and the observer conscious only of the personality, not of the garments.

Specific Types

1. Prominent nose. There are two points which every woman with a large nose must remember about her hats. She cannot wear brimless hats nor hard crowns of any kind without exaggerating the already prominent feature.

With glasses and long chin. For this type a brim which extends at least beyond the glasses and the nose is necessary. A brim which turns up at one side and has some irregularity, as in figures 99 and 100, is best for this type. A straight sailor is too regular of line and makes irregular features more pronounced by contrast.

A decidedly mushroom brim obscures the top half of the face oval until only the lower half (the long nose and chin) remains visible. Therefore a wide, soft crown of irregular line, and a medium-size brim of irregular line and some width, are best for this type of face.

FIGURE 99. Note the Wide Soft Lines of Both Brim and Crown.

With glasses and short chin. Glasses, as we said before, necessitate some brim. A short chin changes the requirements of the type above to a smaller brim and crown. The lines may be practically the same. The crown may be as high, but not as wide.

With receding forehead. This is one of the most difficult types of faces to fit with a becoming hat. As a rule, the headsize is

FIGURE 100. The Brim Extends Out Over the Face before Turning Up. The Handmade Quill Gives Width and Irregularity of Line.

small, yet the lines of the hat need to be soft, rather wide, and irregular. A small rolled or straight brim with a small coronet, which has width and some height, is always becoming. The coronet may be embroidered with soft materials, as ribbonzene or georgette folds, or narrow ribbon. The embroidered material may be draped on loosely. The coronet may be covered with very small flowers or with folds of taffeta or hair braid. A ruffle of velvet or a wired flare of lace will give the same desired effect.

With prominent forehead. A prominent nose and prominent forehead rarely occur together. When they do, they usually belong to a person of strong and marked mental characteristics. If the face is full, wide upturned brims and irregular draped turbans that have not a severe headsize line may be worn. Brims that are wide at the side and narrower at front and back are becoming if there is some irregularity of line. As a rule, a frame has to be shaped and adjusted for each individual of this type.

2. **Small or snub nose.** As a rule, a small snub, or tip-tilted, nose belongs to a little face. The face may take on fat, but it most likely started life small.

Here, more than in other types, the rule of keeping a crown proportionate to the width of the face oval should be followed. This means that the crown should be very little wider and not narrower than the face at its widest point.

With glasses. Small brims very nearly straight or slightly rolled are becoming to this group. Soft ribbon hats that roll from the face are good because they do not form an abrupt turn at the headsize. Tricorns and irregular napoleons are becoming. Larger hats cannot be too extreme in size. They are usually becoming with short or turned-up backs. A short back line balances better with the flat profile than does a wide back.

With low forehead. A girl with a low forehead and a snub nose can almost invariably wear becoming chin-chin hats, rolled sailors, tricorns, and brims of the walking-hat order. Larger hats must have perfectly coördinate lines, usually with a short roll at the back and not too great width anywhere.

FIGURE 101. The Hat in This Figure Has Soft Width with Lifted Lines. This Makes It Becoming to the Wide Face Oval.

With high cheek bones. Hats for a girl with high cheek bones and a small nose take a great deal of study. Small brims with wide, soft trimming; small brims with tam crowns; sailors; and irregular, wide, small hats, are safest and most fitting to the type.

3. Wide face oval. A wide face oval usually needs wide, soft crowns, as cap crowns draped wide from side to side, saddle crowns, two-section crowns, and tam crowns.

With high cheek bones. A wide face with high cheek bones needs an unusual kind of irregularity. The crown must be kept low or there will be an exaggerated kind of oval effect formed by the crown and lower part of the face. There must be width of brim to counterbalance the width of face, usually an up-turned brim. A slash at the side of the brim with added width of ribbon ornament or feather is a good formula. Wide napoleons and continentals are becoming. A girl of this type must be careful of the way she wears her hat. A very slight angle with the brim

FIGURE 102. The Brim of This Hat Is Cut in an Interesting Way to Give Height and Irregularity of Line.

pulled well down on the head is good. A hat worn back on the head with this kind of face becomes grotesque.

With wide, high forehead. A wide face oval and wide forehead invariably mean a large headsize. Together they mean wide, soft crowns, and wide, exaggerated brims with a bend or roll.

FIGURE 103. The Brim of This Design Gives Broken Lines Very Becoming to Many Full Face Ovals.

Slashed brims — that is, irregular, up-turned brims with a slash at the side or side front — give good lines (see figures 103 and 104, Chapter XIII). Only French (slightly rolled) sailors and flat brims with rolled edge or a mushroom effect at the headsize and a straight flange are becoming.

With glasses. A wide face oval with glasses means that there must not be a decided or severe headsize line. Otherwise the formula is the same as for Figure 104 below.

With large headsize and much hair. There is a straight crown which is very becoming to this type when the side crown is softly draped with even folds of fabric. It is generally used on a modified-shepherdess or a walking-hat brim. Brims which are wide and irregular and roll from, rather than turn off, the face are becoming. A big headsize means, of course, a brim proportionately large.

With small nose and chin. A wide face oval with small nose and chin needs soft, wide crowns that are of medium height, as a four-section cap crown, large cap or puffed crown, and some of the crowns made entirely of folds. Small napoleons, irregular turbans, small-brim hats with irregular width in the trimming, and poke brims with transparent maline or lace edges make good frames for this kind of face.

FIGURE 104. The Slashed Front of This Brim Gives Irregularity to Its High Flare.

4. **Narrow face oval.** The hat becoming to the narrow face oval is one that will soften the lines of the face (the features of a narrow face oval have a tendency to be sharp) and shorten the length of the face. Many of the small mushrooms and pokes are becoming. Turned-up brims should come well down over the head before turning. Turbans must be wide and soft with a lower drape or line of folds on one side (see Figure 105).

With very long nose. There is a medium rolled brim with lines between those of a chin-chin and a French sailor which is becoming to this type (see Figures 99 and 101). Fabric crowns

LINE HARMONY

that are draped over the pressed crown, giving softness and some width, are becoming to this type of face. Hats that have very irregular lines, like a modified or cut tricorn, give good brim lines.

With very low forehead. For a long face oval with low forehead the general lines as given in Figure 100, are good. As the crown presents a separate problem, four-section cap crowns pulled low on one side, and regulation cap crowns wide from side to side and draped low at the right side, give good lines for this type.

With long chin. A long face oval with a long chin makes some width in an up-turned hat necessary for balance of line. Mushroom brims are good if they are not severe and if they do not droop decidedly. A brim which droops a great deal shows only hat, a little face, and a long chin.

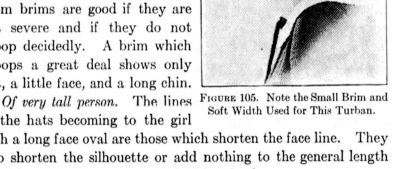

FIGURE 105. Note the Small Brim and Soft Width Used for This Turban.

Of very tall person. The lines of the hats becoming to the girl with a long face oval are those which shorten the face line. They also shorten the silhouette or add nothing to the general length effect, so there is no extra problem involved.

With much hair. This means a long face oval with a large headsize. The brim lines may be the same. They need only be exaggerated and the brim made wider in proportion to the crown.

5. The round face. The hat for a round face oval should be so designed as to add to or lengthen the oval. The crown must always be wider than the face at its widest point. A narrow crown makes the face seem larger.

With snub nose. A snub, or short, nose with a round face means that the hat cannot be too large of brim and cannot turn up too decidedly from the forehead. A brim which extends out an inch or more and then turns up is becoming if it has wide irregularity. Width of brim and lifted line are needed for the full face (see Figure 103).

Care must be exercised not to have the brim turned too high or the line will make the nose seem even smaller.

With glasses. The round face oval with glasses makes it necessary for a hat to have more brim than the other types under this heading.

A brim which rolls decidedly in the back, slightly at the sides, and extends almost straight over the face to about three inches in front and three and one-half or four inches at the side fronts is always good (see Figure 106). Large, soft crowns, irregular brims with width, and only the turned-up brims that have a visor or a headsize roll are becoming to girls or women of this division.

Very small chin. A small chin with a round face presents an added difficulty to the already difficult matter of selecting a becoming hat. This particular set of features usually belong to a short person and the hat should have lines which add length to the silhouette. The accepted means of obtaining height are not possible because they would make a top-heavy effect in proportion to the face, and a high trimming, or an extremely high crown or brim will make the chin smaller by comparison.

Draped turbans of the modified Hindu type (see Figure 105), but with a small brim or visor, small brims with wide draped crowns, and close-fitting tricorns or napoleons are becoming to this classification. There must be no drooping lines to cut either

FIGURE 106. Width of Brim, Short Back, and Rolled Front Make This Style Becoming to Many Women.

profile or silhouette line. The effect is rather that of height without high trimming.

With very high forehead. A round face with a very high forehead of course means a large face with an oval both high and wide.

A large, well-fitting headsize is always one of the first requisites. The hat should be worn well down over the head. The crown must be wide and soft and of average height. The brim may be a sailor, a slightly drooping mushroom, or a modified tricorn of low rather than high lines. Full crown trimmings, as flowers or feathers, make good balance with the face lines.

Mode of Hairdressing Adapted to Types

1. As it affects the facial contour. The manner of dressing the hair may do much to change and soften the lines of the face. There are very few women who can wear their hair pulled straight back from the face without any softness. Women who have smooth skin and beautiful, lustrous, not extremely soft hair, often adopt this severity of line and wear the extreme clothing and jewels which are accessories to the bizarre effect that they desire.

To the average woman, in nine hundred and ninety-five out of a thousand cases, who is neither extremely beautiful nor extremely plain, a soft arrangement of the hair is vastly more becoming. It is too obvious for detailed remark that some width at the sides and over the ears softens and widens the contour of the thin face, that a round face needs a higher head dress, that a high forehead needs the hair pulled low in front or parted at one side to obscure part of the forehead, and that usually the hair should be combed straight back from a low forehead to take advantage of all the possible length of oval.

2. As it affects the profile. As the old Greek conception of facial perfection was a straight profile and an irregular head line

LINE HARMONY 197

(men with a head wide from the face to the back of the head, wide spacing from eye to ear; and women with regular features, who dressed their hair in a Psyche knot), so the hair arrangement today should be made to soften the profile where the features are sharp or too decided, and to exaggerate their size where the features are not sufficiently pronounced, in order to achieve, as far as possible, the Grecian ideal.

3. **As it affects the hat**. As a general rule, a hat is more becoming when the hair shows just a little on the forehead and at the sides.

A hat which is worn so that it shows no hair is apt to be disfiguring.

A large knot of hair requires a hat adjusted to fit the hair. When the hair is worn in a large knot on top of the head, the crown must be deeper than for the usual head dress. To adjust the crown properly, allow at least one inch at the headsize of any crown pattern.

When the hair is worn in a large knot at the back of the head, the headsize of the brim and the crown headsize should be shaped in a decided oblong. If a pressed crown foundation is used, it will need to be raised. Rip the headsize wire. Stitch a bias strip of elastic net or buckram to the headsize edge. Trim the lower edge of this strip evenly and wire it. Add an extra inch to the headsize of the crown pattern to allow fullness for the crown and hair.

Never plan to adjust the hair for a certain hat. Only a lady of leisure has time to do this. Adjust the hat to the hair.

To put on a hat properly, catch the headsize of the hat over the top half of the knot, pull the hat well down in front, and tilt it slightly down on the right side. For a bob pull the hat over the back of the head, down in front, and tilt it to the right in the same way.

Only the girl with perfect features can wear a hat straight. A slight angle preserves better balance of line with irregular features.

QUESTIONS

1. What is meant by "line" in millinery?
2. In what way is the industrial art of millinery correlated with the fine art of sculpture?
3. Do the general principles of line in hats change with the fashions?
4. What is the object to be attained in choosing the lines of a hat for an individual?
5. Name one of the important things to remember in choosing a hat for a girl with glasses.
6. Give the general rules in selecting a hat for a girl with a
   a. Prominent nose.
   b. Small nose.
   c. Wide face oval.
   d. Narrow face oval.
   e. Round face.

FIGURE 107. These reproductions of hats are used through the courtesy of the C. A. Loewen Company, 37 South Wabash Avenue, Chicago, Illinois, from which information may be obtained.

FIGURE 108. These reproductions of hats are used through the courtesy of the C. A. Loewen Company, 37 South Wabash Avenue, Chicago, Illinois, from which information may be obtained.

FIGURE 109. These reproductions of hats are used through the courtesy of the C. A. Loewen Company, 37 South Wabash Avenue, Chicago, Illinois, from which information may be obtained.

FIGURE 110. These reproductions of hats are used through the courtesy of the C. A. Loewen Company, 37 South Wabash Avenue, Chicago, Illinois, from which information may be obtained.

FIGURE 111. These reproductions of hats are used through the courtesy of the C. A. Loewen Company, 37 South Wabash Avenue, Chicago, Illinois, from which information may be obtained.

Figure 112.

FIGURE 113.

Figure 114.

FIGURE 115.

FIGURE 116.

CPSIA information can be obtained at www.ICGtesting.com
Printed in the USA
LVOW100023030112

261982LV00001B/4/P